T0094703

Betrayal

A Member of the Kennedy Honor Guard Speaks

Hugh Clark

with William Matson Law

Published by:
Trine Day LLC
PO Box 577
Walterville, OR 97489
1-800-556-2012
www.TrineDay.com
publisher@TrineDay.net

Library of Congress Control Number: 2016953402

Clark, Hugh and Law, William Matson —1st ed.
p. cm.
Includes references and index.
Epub (ISBN-13) 978-1-63424-094-9
Mobi (ISBN-13) 978-1-63424-095-6
Print (ISBN-13) 978-1-63424-093-2
1. Kennedy, John F. -- (John Fitzgerald), -- 1917-1963 -- Assassination 2. Hu-
bert A. Clark -- 1944-. 3. Bethesda Naval Hospital. 4. Presidential Honor Guard
-- John F. Kennedy. I. Clark, Hugh and Law, William Matson. II. Title

FIRST EDITION
10 9 8 7 6 5 4 3 2 1

Printed in the USA
Distribution to the Trade by:
Independent Publishers Group (IPG)
814 North Franklin Street
Chicago, Illinois 60610
312.337.0747
www.ipgbook.com

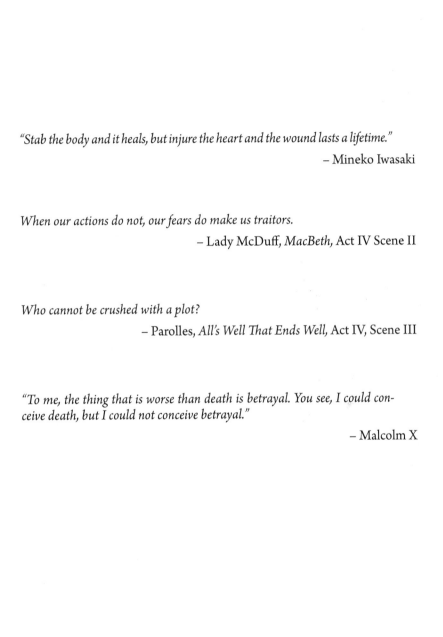

"Stab the body and it heals, but injure the heart and the wound lasts a lifetime."

– Mineko Iwasaki

When our actions do not, our fears do make us traitors.

– Lady McDuff, *MacBeth*, Act IV Scene II

Who cannot be crushed with a plot?

– Parolles, *All's Well That Ends Well*, Act IV, Scene III

"To me, the thing that is worse than death is betrayal. You see, I could conceive death, but I could not conceive betrayal."

– Malcolm X

I couldn't believe what I was hearing. As the speaker continued, I felt my blood pressure rise. Three speakers on the panel discussed the entry of a casket into the morgue at Bethesda Naval Hospital. That casket contained the body of the 35th President of the United States, John F. Kennedy, in the aftermath of Kennedy's assassination in Dallas, Texas, on November 22, 1963.

The speaker said, "I am going to tell you the truth about the casket. I have it from a highly placed source that the casket contained oxygen tanks and weighed 2500 pounds."

The room was full of attentive listeners from all around the country who had come to Dallas to gain knowledge of Kennedy's assassination. Still one of the biggest mysteries the world has ever known. I knew what the panelist was saying was not true.

I didn't know who his highly placed source was, but the panelist had been misled. How do I know? I was there. My name is Hugh Clark, and I was one of the six military men who took the ornate display casket into the Bethesda morgue and later took Kennedy's remains to Arlington National Cemetery.

Contents

Foreword

The Devil Is In The Details

Hugh Clark, is not yet a name known by those who prowl the dark corridors of assassination research, yet it will be. The term "honor" is a concept whose meaning these days has dwindled like a dying ember from a once roaring fire. It shouldn't be. The Merriam-Webster definition of the word "honor" states: "a good name or public esteem," "merited respect," "one whose worth brings respect," and "an evidence or symbol of distinction." In the military, an honor guard is a person who exemplifies the highest standards and conduct of his military branch. An honor guard is known as "guardian of the colors" and as such displays and escorts the national flag on ceremonial occasions. Churches of the Anglican Communion and the Methodist movement have the tradition of an honor guard at the funeral of an ordained elder, in which all other ordained elders present "guard the line" between the door of the church and the grave.

Hugh Clark was an honor guard and served this country in that noble position. In 1963, he was one of six men whose duty it was to deliver the casket carrying the body of John F. Kennedy into the Bethesda morgue and later, to render his remains to Arlington National Cemetery. He was in fact guarding the line between the door of the church and the grave. Hugh Clark was also a witness to events that day which would change the course of history. Over the next fifty years the importance of what he witnessed would remain buried, but not forgotten. As he recalls "I felt I had been a cog in the wheel in the history of that event." In 2014, an event occurred which would alter his life again.

The details of what Clark saw on that day will confirm what most of us have come to suspect; a massive cover-up was undertaken at the highest levels of government. From his vantage point, Hugh Clark unravels the details of this deception, and the devil is in the details.

Among all the literature written about the Kennedy Assassination there are very few personal narratives. This is one of the important ones. Hugh Clark has a story to tell and I for one am relieved that he has put down on paper what amounts to a inside look at one of history's darkest moments. In 1963 Hugh Clark was an honor guard and he is still an honor guard; guarding the truth. In my view he is and will always be an honorable man.

–Saint John Hunt
Fort Lauderdale, Florida, 2016

At home today in Georgia.

Chapter One

BUILDING MY CHARACTER

I was born August 14, 1944 at the Bonnett Hospital in Paterson, New Jersey.

My given name is Hubert Allonza, but my family called me Papa. I had four brothers, and six sisters. My dad was a pastor, and my mother was a housewife. I grew up at 160 12th Avenue, between the railroad tracks and Godwin Avenue. My childhood was normal, a lot of fun, as one can imagine, with eleven kids in the house. We never were at a loss for playmates.

James Jr. was the oldest, like a father figure for me. He has doctorates in both education and theology. He's also a pastor. Next in line was Samuel, who was like my mentor. He went into the Marine Corp at the age of seventeen and I guess you can say he was the fighter in the family – he would not back down, ever. My older sister, Alberta, was the mother of the house when my mother would go to work. Then there was my brother, Ben, who we call Dixie Drifter, because he was also in the Marine Corp. Next was my sister, Evangeline, who was very spirited and broke my nose as a kid playing softball. That's why I don't play softball anymore with women.

My brother Joe, a year older than I, they called the Mayor of East Elmhurst. He would always stand out on the corner with three people in the neighborhood. Then there was me, who was full of mischief. The drunks would come by at night and I would throw potatoes at them. They couldn't figure out where the potatoes were coming from.

My younger sister, Mary, was a school kid. My sister Henrietta, was a librarian who kept to herself and got married. Then there was my sister Lois, a great sister and a lot of fun. She also went into the Navy for twenty six years and came out as a Chief Warrant officer. Then there was my sister, Frances, who died at an early age – thirty two, thirty three. She was like the baby, but a lot of fun, a really good cook, especially chitlins, that she always made and all of us loved visiting her house. But, as a family, I think we were very close. That's one thing my dad and mom always instilled in us, was family. Being from a large family helped me to work as a team player. If you messed with one of us at a fight, you messed with all of us. We were known at the 12th Avenue gang.

Because my dad was a pastor and moved around from church to church, he was transferred to Westchester County in New York from Patterson, New Jersey. It was more freestyle living, a small town where everyone knew each other. In grade school I got into sports, which I loved, including soccer and football. That's where I really became a sports guy, especially with football. I loved football and played at my avenue. From there, I went onto junior high, where I really saw an opportunity to play junior varsity football. Then, just when I became eligible for varsity, my dad got transferred again to New York City. During this time, my dad was the Dean of Robert C. Lawson's Christ Bible Institute, which was located in Harlem. Based on what other pastors said, he was the best teacher that they ever met.

My dad was born in Trinidad, in the West Indies, and my mom was born in South Carolina. I remember conversations, especially when all of us would gather around the dinner table. My mom would be cooking. Once everybody had the opportunity to sit down and start eating, I always wondered how they met since my father was from Trinidad and my mom was from South Carolina. Because my dad was a young pastor, normally they have outings and picnics. My dad met my mom at a fish fry and we always thought that was a big laugh. But they raised all of us as a happy family. Mom was the disciplinarian. My father really didn't like disciplining the kids. If something went wrong in the house, my mother lined us all up in the dining room. If she came home from work and the house was a mess, we didn't clean up after playing all day, she would line everybody up starting with the oldest and all the way down to the baby. Everybody got a whack and we used to think, "This lady's trying to kill us." Whenever we would say, "Mom, please, please, please," she would always make a comment, "I'm doing this because I love you!" That would confuse us as kids. If she loved us why was she doing this? We couldn't understand it at the time. But as we got older, we understood. She was a great mom and a great provider. One of the things that made us kids really feel close to mom was that my dad was in the ministry, and he was always traveling. Whenever any of us got sick, mom was there. She had this idea that if one of us got the chicken pox, or one of us got the measles, she'd put us all in the room together to make sure that everybody got it at the same time. Believe it or not, it worked. Mom was always there to take care of us.

My dad had one of the most distinguishing features, half of his hair was black and the other half was gray. All the way down the middle. He was very distinguished looking. And he had this one tooth on the right side that whenever he laughed, we could always see a gold tooth. Whenever he was angry, we could never understand what he was saying because he had a very heavy British accent, and "bloody" this and "bloody" that was all we could make out. The first time I ever remember going to the beach, my dad would take me out into the water and the wave would go out, and my dad would walk out with me on his shoulder, and then he would put me down and I would try to run back to shore before that wave caught up to me. That's how I learned how to swim, and I just thought he was the greatest dad in the world.

I was born in the 40's and lived in a very mixed neighborhood. Some neighbors were white. We had a Chinese laundry two doors down from us. My best friend at that time was a white kid named Bobby who lived down the block, and I used to help him with his paper route. We'd buy White Tower hamburgers after we finished or he would buy mine as my payment. It was just a good time. Right across the street was a barbershop, Tony's Barbershop. There was a candy store right across the street from where I grew up in Patterson, New Jersey. Living in such a neighborhood taught me respect for others.

We always had this big, big maple tree in front of the house and we would all sit out on the stoop. At least once a week a man with an accordion would come by, and we would sit out, all eleven of us, on a stoop, and he would play this accordion and we would all sing, "Yes, Jesus loves me. Yes, Jesus loves me. Yes, Jesus loves me, for the bible tells me so." Then he would give us each a penny. We'd run across the street and back in those days a penny would buy a handful of peppermints. Even though we didn't like waiting, we would sit out on the stoop anyway and sing that song to get that penny.

Living in an integrated neighborhood may have been unusual for folks living in those times, but not for me or my family. Back then, everybody on the block got along. There were so many kids on the block. Nobody would dare come to our block and mess with us because there were 11 of us. Our next door neighbor had three kids, down the block neighbors had four more kids, and then across the street lived five more kids. So we had a lot of kids on our block. The block was longer than a city block, from Godwin Avenue all the way down the railroad tracks. Once you crossed the railroad tracks, we were not on our block anymore. If I went off the block, being a little kid, and because I had older brothers, no one would dare touch me. I don't ever remember leaving the block without one of my oldest siblings except for one time when I really got in trouble.

My mother went downtown to work, and I told myself, (I think I was five years old), "I'm going to follow her." I followed my mother all the way downtown which was maybe three or four miles away. She didn't know I was behind her but apparently she got on the bus at some point, but I didn't see her and I got lost. My mother did what she had to do and came back home and her first question was, "Where is Hubert?" Nobody knew. Meanwhile, I was wandering around downtown, trying to find my way home and the entire block was out looking for me. My mom had called the police and the police were out looking for me too. Finally, the police saw me wandering, or they had put out a description of me and they found me and put me in the back of a police car, bought me a bag of peanuts, and by that time I had soiled my pants and I smelled really bad.

I wasn't scared until I saw my mother. When the police pulled up in front of the house, the entire block was out there, all the kids and all the parents. When the police took me out of that police car, everybody was cheering. My mother grabbed me. She didn't want to do anything in front of the cops. She took me upstairs and cleaned me up. Before she did, she sat me down in the dining room and she lined up all my sisters and brothers against the wall and beat them. I just sat there thinking, "She's going to kill me."

After, we moved from New Jersey when I was a teenager and moved to Mamaroneck, Westchester County. I really got into sports, playing basketball, soccer, and softball. I was always a fast runner. There wasn't a lot of drama in Westchester County in Mamaroneck, because the town was so small and I was getting ready for junior high school because I wanted to play junior varsity league football. As soon as I graduated from that junior high, I tried out for the JV team and but my father got transferred again to East Elmhurst, Queens. That really upset me.

Mamaroneck was more like a city. The only thing that they really did was play basketball, and baseball. They didn't have the activities or the sport activities that Westchester County had, because Westchester County was more rural. The junior high and high school had big athletic fields: a 440 yard track, baseball, softball, and football fields.

The first school that I went to was PS 127, where the only major sport that I really played was basketball. That's when I became friends with other kids in the neighborhood. We were all in the same class and had a basketball team we called the Celtics, and we just beat everybody. I don't know how many trophies I had just from playing basketball.

We had one thing that the other schools in Westchester didn't have, a recreation center. Every Tuesday, Wednesday and Thursday night, we played basketball and other games such as ping-pong. I concerned myself with basketball and I really became good at it.

During the summer, we had basketball tournaments where other teams would come from all over the city. We had one pro athlete, Ray Felix. We participated in the Ray Felix tournaments which we won every year, competing with schools from all over the city. That's when I started learning all the other school basketball plays that were really great. Guys like Connie Hawkins and Roger Brown went on to the pros.

I graduated from PS 127 and because of a quirk of fate, went on to the high school of fashion in industries, specializing in tailoring, pattern making, designs, ladies clothes, and men's clothes.

A friend of mine who was a year ahead had told me and a couple of other guys, about this specialized school. We were getting ready to go to high school and we were all trying to figure out where we could go. Our teacher said, "You have to take a test to get in." We said, "Okay." We went down. We took the test. We passed.

One of the things that I noticed when we went to Jervis, (that was the name of the school) was how many girls there were. I was 14 or 15, and I liked girls. I was always interested my appearance. I tried to model myself after my dad because as a pastor, he always wore three-piece suits. I always loved the vest that had a pocket watch with a chain that came across the vest. Whenever he would be getting dressed, I would be in that room sitting on a bed watching him in his starched shirts. My dad was very polished and I always wanted to dress like him.

When I graduated from the 9th grade, I went right into that high school which was in Manhattan. I had to get up, take a bus, and take the subway to school. During my first year I was amazed at the diversity especially the pretty girls, black, white, Spanish, Italian, Indian, and Chinese. Oh man, I was in heaven!

The girls that I wanted to date were all a year or two years ahead of me and they wouldn't have anything to do with a freshman. As soon as basketball season started, I made the basketball team. I didn't have any problems finding a girlfriend after that.

The cheerleaders and the student body would come to most of the home games. Good players got a lot of floor time. My first girlfriend in high school, her name was Alexis. I remember she would always sit in the front row. Whenever I would shoot the ball, she would jump up and cheer. Whether I made it or not, she would jump up and cheer and that's what caught my eye. After the game, I would go take a shower and when I came out, she was always standing there.

Although I liked girls, I was awkward around them and didn't know what to say. I remember coming home and asking my older brothers, "What do you say and how should the conversation go?" I went to my sisters and they would guide me through and I'd always go to school the next day and try out what they had said. If it worked, I would stick with it. If it didn't, I'd come home for more education.

My sisters would tell me, "Just be nice and open the door. Make sure you open the door. Don't curse. Don't spit around her. Don't be rough. Don't be afraid to hold her hand. Make sure you sit with her at lunch if you can. Make sure you complement her. Not too much, but just complement her."

Through high school I had a joyous time because I got involved in not just playing basketball but playing handball and running track. I remember the parties at people's houses, because I met people from all over the city, the Bronx, Brooklyn, Manhattan, and Staten Island.

All the kids at the school knew how to sew. We were making our own suits. We were making pants. We were making two-piece suits. We were making three-piece suits.

If I wanted a pattern for a suit, I would tell a guy who was a pattern maker. I would say, "If you make me a pattern for this kind of suit, I'll make you a suit." So he'd make the pattern and I would make him a suit. That's how good I was. I was going to make this my career.

Every day you would see somebody in some beautiful outfits, especially girls. They would make all different types of clothes. They would design their own clothes. There were guys that made shoes. There were guys that made hats. If you wanted a hat, somebody would make a hat for you.

I would make a suit every two weeks. All I needed was three and a half yards of material. The last suit I made for myself, I stayed up all night. My mom and dad bought me a sewing machine and I had all the things that I needed. I had my yard stick. I had my thread. I could make button holes. I could make you a suit because in class that's what we did. So whatever you did in class, you brought home with you and would do the same thing at home. It was a navy blue suit with cuffs.

I got home from school. I put my pattern down. I cut it out. I basted it, using this wooden frame. I did not go to sleep until the following day because I wanted to wear that suit to school in the morning. When I got up, I had that suit and I pressed it out. I already had my light blue shirt and my tie. I wore that suit to school the next day. Once I made a suit, it's very easy to make others. Making my own clothes made me feel independent and taught me to be task oriented.

I can still sew. If you put a machine in front of me and if I had to make a button hole, I would know how to do it. It's something I have never forgotten and to this day I can put cuffs in pants and stitch up a tear. If you put it in front of me I can fix it. I did it for three years, and I had every intention of going to FIT, which was the Fashion Institute of Technology. In my last year of high school I went to school a week and I worked a week. I was fortunate enough to be assigned to Saks Fifth Avenue.

I got paid a wage for working at Saks Fifth Avenue and I was able to buy shoes. When I worked at Saks, I couldn't go in there in dungarees even as a worker. I had to dress sharp. I worked in the tailor shop or the alterations shop where I honed my skills. I had every intention of going on and opening up a line because I had become that good. The best tailors in high school were the Italian students, they could sew.

I remember Vido Pazentino who could sew by hand faster than some people could sew with a machine. He had been sewing since he was five years old and he was a great tailor. If I said to Vito, "I want to make this blazer," he would say, "No problem, no problem." He would help me out and before two days of class were over, I would have my blazer done.

I made quality stuff. If I bought material, if I saw a piece of clothing in a magazine I liked, I said, "This is what I want to make." I would go to one of the pattern guys. He would measure me and make the pattern. I would buy the material and make the clothing.

My last year of high school, I was still playing basketball, and our high school team played at Madison Square Gardens. We got knocked out in the first round, but that was the first time that the school had been to Madison Square Gardens in thirty years. As graduation grew closer and closer, we had an awards assembly for the entire school. Students received letters for best attendance and for all the teams they were on.

I got team letters for basketball, for track, and for hand ball. I had 14 letters and it seemed like every time I would go up I would get another award for something else. Then came the prom which was most exciting. I was chosen king of the prom. The queen of the prom was a gorgeous Chinese girl, Peggy Chen. At the prom the king and queen's chairs were up front on the stage. We also had the first dance together. My girlfriend at the time, Lorraine, didn't like that.

When I graduated from high school, Lorraine and I had dated probably a year and a half. We were close. She lived in St. Albans, Queens and I lived in East Elmhurst, Queens. I had to take a bus and a train to get to her house. She would come and visit and I would go and visit. High school was one of the best times of my life because I really enjoyed it. I met a lot of people, guys from all over the City and to this day I could probably name them. My best friend at the time was Ronnie. He went to Brooklyn Tech and we are still best friends.

Lorraine and I dated all through high school. We went all over to parties and met people from all over the place. If there was a party in the Bronx, we would go to the Bronx and if there was a party in Queens, they would come to Queens. All my neighborhood friends are still friends today after almost 60 years.

The day I received the gold shield and moved up to Detective.
I am wearing a suit I made.

Chapter Two

SERVING MY COUNTRY

I had intentions of going on to college. I had a basketball scholarship to Clark University. When I got out of high school, my brothers had come home on leave and I saw them in their uniforms. That was it. I said, "Oh no. I've got to get into the military," because girls were flocking all over them. I wanted to go, but I didn't want to go into the Marine Corps. I didn't want to go into the Army.

I was begging my dad at the time. I said, "Dad, please, I want to go in the Navy." The recruiter was right down the street from my school. So one day after school I went to the recruiter and asked, "I want to join the Navy and what do I have to do?" I was about to graduate, had turned 17, and he said, "Well, fill out the paperwork and bring it back and do all this stuff." I graduated in June, and I hadn't even told my dad or my mother. It wasn't until the recruiter said, "Listen. Because you're only 17, your father's going to have to sign it."

My parents wanted me to go college and get that education. My oldest brother, James, was in the Air Force. My brother next to him, Sam, was in the Marine Corps. My brother Ben was in the Marine Corps. I wanted to go into the Navy and see the world. When the recruiter told me that my Dad had to sign the paperwork, I said, "What? Are you kidding?" That was the longest ride home I ever had in my life because how was I going to swing this?

Because I was the baby boy, my mom and dad wanted me home since all my other brothers were in the military, and my brother Joe couldn't go into the military as he had been hurt in an accident. They wanted one son home to go to school and get an education. When I got home, my mom was in bed. I said, "Mom. Listen. I want to go into the service. I really don't know what I want to do now. I'm not ready to go to college." She understood because she had all the girls there. She was easy.

She said, "How are you going to tell your father?" My dad was an educator who believed in education. I said, "I don't know. Can you help me?" She looked at me and because I was 17 then and she said "No. You're on your own. You're going to have to do this on your own."

I knew that my dad wanted me home because I was his baby boy. He and I were always close. Vietnam was brewing. Even though we weren't in a war, it was brewing; we heard little rumblings about it. So he was concerned.

When that recruiter said, "Listen, in order for you to get on the bus, or in order for you to go to boot camp, you're going to have to bring your father down here to sign these papers," I thought to myself, "Oh my God." I said, "Well, can my mother sign them?" He said, "No, it has to be your dad because you're not 18." I was stranded.

So I went to my Dad and said, "You know, Dad. I signed up to go into the navy. This is what I really want to do. I'm really not ready for college. If I go into the navy, I'll get the GI bill. I'll be able to go to school for free and they'll pay for it."

My Dad looked at me and said, "You need to stay here and go to school and get a good education, get a good job, raise a family. You never know what's going to break out in the world."

I said, "I understand, but there's nothing going on right now. I'm not going to be in a war zone."

Then my mom said, "He really wants to do this. It's going to help him grow up. It's going to help him be a better person. Let him be away from home for a little while and it will make him become more independent, get stronger." She convinced him. This decision changed my life.

When it came time to go and meet the recruiter, my dad came down with me. When the recruiter saw us, he said, "Bishop, you got to sign here."

My dad started crying. He said, "I don't know. This is my baby boy."

I'm standing there, "Dad, please." I said, "Please, dad, please." I said, "Dad, the bus is out there."

The recruiter was pleading with him. "Bishop, it's going to be okay. He's going to be with a lot of good guys and we're going to take care of him. We're going to make a man out of him and he's going to be serving his country."

I said, "Dad, the bus is out there. They're going to leave me."

I started sweating and the recruiter said, "Bishop, it's going to be okay. You'll see. When he comes back home, you're not even going to recognize him." Finally, he signed the paper. I gave him a bear hug and I was on that bus. I got on that bus going down to White Hall Street, to get my physical. I was on my own. I didn't know what to expect, but I was looking forward to the adventure.

There were at least thirty guys on the bus, white, black, Asian, and we were all going to the same place, though not for the same military service. Once we got to Whitewall Street, we took our physicals and were sworn in.

I just felt this rush of excitement. From that point, we were assigned, and put in an area where Navy, Army, Air Force, Marines were separated. Then we were taken to LaGuardia Airport with about 20 other recruits.

At the airport, we waited for our plane, and once the plane arrived there were other guys from other parts of the city. The plane was full with the navy recruits that were going to Great Lakes, Illinois. When we landed in Illinois, there was a bus waiting for us. When we got off the plane outside the terminal, we all boarded the bus. I thought, "I wonder if we're all going to be in the same company, or what is it going to be like?" By that time there had to be a couple a hundred guys that had come from all over the United States to Great Lakes or to the airport, and we all boarded buses, sat back, waiting, wondering what this experience was going to be like?

What is it going to be like? Who is this guy? Where is he from? But there wasn't a lot of conversation between the recruits, just a lot of anticipation. I forgot how long the bus ride was, but I remember we arrived at Camp Moffet, that was the receiving depot.

Before we even got off the bus, I saw the company commander, either a chief or first class petty officer. The bus doors opened up, and this guy got on. I don't remember his name because he never told us. He said, "When I give the signal or when I give the order, I don't want to see anything but asses and elbows, getting off this bus and falling into a straight line. No talking, no nothing."

He was a big white man. He appeared to be in great shape, so I figured he must be the PT instructor. Everybody was so nervous; nobody wanted to make a mistake. There was no talking, and when he said "Move," we got on that bus in less than a minute. Later, we were all off the bus, and had our bags by our feet. He said, "I don't know how many of you people know your left from your right, but by the time you leave here you're going to know that and a lot more."

The he said, "Now as you follow the guy in front of you, and the guy in front, you follow me." He took us into the recruit depot, and he said, "Now strip down." We stripped down and stood there naked.

Everybody was so frightened because we didn't want this guy to come up to us and yell at us. So everybody just followed orders, nobody looked at anyone else. The first thing we did was took a 30 second shower, and dressed in skivvy shorts, tops and bottoms. We got haircuts; in essence they shaved our heads.

I didn't care. I figure that was all a part of the process. I think for the most part everybody was just ready. Whatever this guy said to do, whenever he said go, we just followed directions. Once we got our heads shaved, we got in line and were issued clothing. As we went through the line, we gave our size; small, medium, or large. It wasn't size 32; it was small, medium and large.

I weighed about 130 pounds, so I immediately took size medium, and medium was pretty good. At the end of the line we got sea bags. We put in what they told us, exactly what they wanted us to put on: dungarees, a dungaree shirt, a white hat and boondockers. Boondockers were like desert boots, but leather. We got socks, pants and underwear. Everything we needed we got: toothbrush, toothpaste, hats, dungaree jacket. Everything was put into the sea bag, except for what they've told us they wanted us to put on. Once all that was done, everybody lined up to form our company. We stood there at attention, with our sea bags by our feet and the company commander said, "Okay, stay in here. Your company commander will be coming to pick you up and take you to your barracks." We must have stood there for maybe half an hour until our company commander showed up, First Class Petty Officer Johnson.

Officer Johnson was about 5' 11 ½," but stocky. He introduced himself. Nobody said anything. "When I speak to you it's: aye, aye, sir." He packed us all up, we put our sea bags on our shoulders, all 103 of us in the company. Believe it or not, I was the only black guy in the entire company and everybody else was from the South.

We now arrived at Camp Moffet and Officer Johnson told us, "This is going to be what we are doing at Camp Moffet," meaning we are going to be testing. He was civil but he was in charge and he was not a guy to mess with. He explained, "This is why you are here, we are going to teach you, you are going to be men – you came here as boys – but when you leave here you are going to be men. All you gentlemen that think you cannot hack this, step out right now." He said, "This is not a picnic. When you leave here you are going to be ready to go to sea, go to school or you may be on the destroyer, a carrier. You aren't drafted, you signed up to be in the Navy, this is a man's navy, this is not for the faint of heart, you are going to learn a lot, you are going to be expected to learn a lot and we are going to expect you to act like men. There is no room in this man's navy for kids." I think out of the 100, three guys stepped forward and said, "I did not sign up for this. I did not think it was going to be like that."

Then he called someone on the phone who came over and got these recruits who went back to the recruit deck where we arrived. Then he went on with his speech, "This is what we are going to do, we are going to be here for three weeks. You are going to learn military procedure. This is what is going to be expected of you, what we expect from you and this is what you can expect from us."

It was not to make us feel comfortable, but to let us know that we were in the military now, and we were not to do anything unless we were told to do it. It was all about following directions. Officer Johnson said, "If you follow directions you will be okay. If you do not follow directions, you are going to find yourself in a bad place." I followed directions to the tee, because one of the things that I thought at that time was, "Damn I am the only black guy here. I am not going to mess this up."

Officer Johnson went on to say, "There is no color, there is no religion, there is no room for any of that crap. You are in the navy. This is one unit and we are going to act like one unit. If you follow directions, you should not have any problems. If you do not follow directions, you are going to have major problems." Everybody was looking straight ahead. He said, "Does anybody have any questions?" Nobody raised a hand.

Later, when I looked in the mirror, I said, "I made it and I am going to make the most of it." One of Officer Johnson's phrases was, "Just make sure you are squared away at all times." Squared away means that you are clean, that your clothes are neat and clean, your shoes look polished and that you follow directions. I made up my mind right then, that was who I was. I am sure all the other guys made up their minds and thought the same thing.

I had a bald head, I had no mustache and I looked like I was maybe fourteen years old. I had not even started shaving yet and one of the things Officer Johnson said was, "I expect you to be clean-shaven at all times. Your bunk will be made at all times. There will be no sitting on the bunk, no lying on the bunk and these are the rules. If I catch you deviating from those rules it is going to be a problem." I made sure I had no problems with the commanding officers dictates.

We were at Camp Moffet for three weeks. This was almost a staging area to weed out those men who were not able to adjust to the military life. When it was time to go across the road, we had lost another 10 guys.

Of those ten guys, some had slashed their wrists. Some had jumped out the window. Some had wet their beds. Others were unable to just follow simple directions. When we crossed the road, we were more or less locked in to really following what the company commander was saying.

That first night, I think we got to the barracks about 8:00. By the time we finished up, it must have been after 1:00 in the morning. We had picked up our clothes, got our shaved heads and by the time we got to bed, it had to be 2:30 in the morning. We got to bed and then the lights went on. It was 6:00 in the morning. The Company Commander picked up a garbage can and threw it down the middle of the squad bay to shock us.

We got dressed; we brushed our teeth. Then we waited. Then we fell outside and went to breakfast. Company Commander Johnson told us, "When you finish breakfast and you leave the mess hall, go to stand." The first guy would go stand in the spot and everybody would form around that guy. Whatever order that we started out in, that's the order that he wanted us to be in when everybody finished breakfast. We were all lined up outside in a company setting. Then he would come and pick us up. We would march back to the barracks.

All these years later, I can still hear Johnson saying, "I don't want to see nothing but assess and elbows." We jumped out of bed and we stood at attention in front of our bunks. That was the first morning at Camp Moffet.

The second day there, we got these little blue handbooks. That was called the Navy manual. If we were the first outside, we pulled that manual out of our pocket and put it up in front of our face. We were standing outside, looking around watching this. We had our faces in that manual because we had to study that manual.

We hadn't received any rifles while we were at Camp Moffet. What Officer Johnson did was to take us out to what was referred to as "the grinder," an asphalt parade field. Once we were settled with our clothes and making up our beds and going through the basic introduction speech, he took us out to this grinder, and lined us all up in rows. He said, "I need a guide-on." And he said, "Who wants to be a guide-on?" I didn't even know what the hell that was. I raised my hand. It was a flag pole about seven feet long and it had our company flag on it. Our company was company 372. He gave me the guide-on and I was put on the right side, up front of the company, to keep them in line.

So whenever we were marching, I was always the guide-on. Nobody got in front of me. Nobody got beside me. They were always behind me and the petty officer of the company who was in charge of the company when the company commander wasn't there. He was a white guy named Paul. The company commander would take us out to the grinder and he would teach the company the basic, right face, left face, about face.

The number one thing we did every day was calisthenics. Five guys got weeded out from the calisthenics or they were put on the fat brigade. If we couldn't cut it or if we were overweight, we would run in place and we would have to run around the ground. I would have to put the flag at port arms, and I would be in front of the company. Company Commander Johnson would do all the exercises with us. He would be out front with us and he would run with us on the side. He would be shouting, "One two three four, one two three four, one two three four, one two three four." We had to be in step, "One two three four, one two three four, one two three four." There would be four across and four back. Then we would have the first platoon and we would have the second platoon. There were two platoons consisting of 95 guys.

After three weeks, we "crossed the road" to our new barracks – Camp Geiger.

Camp Moffet was a wooden barracks. It was tough to clean the floors because it was all wood floors and it had stains on them and we had to get down and scrub them, scrub them, scrub them, but Camp Geiger was all brick. It was brick like stone floors, steel bunk beds but it was completely different. There were three floors in the barracks and there was a company on each floor of those barracks. We were on the second floor of the barracks, company 372.

We had made it across the road, so things were a little more relaxed, but not the discipline. Commander Johnson wasn't yelling as much, because we were kind of locked into what we needed to do, what we were supposed to do, and as long as we followed directions, it was okay. But if one guy messed up, he would tell us in a minute whether we were marching, whether we were doing calisthenics, to drop down. Because I had the guide on, holding the flag, there were times that I would just stand there because I wasn't supposed to lay the guide on down. But if one guy messed up, Commander Johnson would turn to me and say, "Put that god damn guide-on down, get down there." So I put that guide-on on the ground and we started doing push-ups. One, down one, down two, down three, and that made everybody pissed off. A couple of guys – if he said right face or left face or whatever – would mess up and they did it more than once. Johnson would say, "God damn it, company get down. Get out there, here we go, down one, down two." We would have to do 20 push-ups.

If we were doing calisthenics, one of the things we hated to do, were those bend and thrust, where we would go down and squat and then we had to kick our legs out and then come back up, and then stand up and then go back down and do it again. If one guy messed up, if we weren't in sync, he'd drop us down in a minute.

Guys would roll over and lie on their backs, and Sargent Johnson would be walking around watching us and he would say something like, "God damn it, get up, get up!" And then he'd single a guy out the guy that was messing up and put him in the front. He would tell us, "This is why you do get to do it over, this guy right here." He was trying to make us act like a unit. We never retaliated against a fellow if he screwed up. When the drill instructor would leave, we would be by ourselves. Some guys would say, "Goddamn man, why didn't you get this right?" Some of the guys walked like they were behind a plow, but we were pretty good up to a point. I think my fifth week at boot camp is when shit started to happen.

I was the only black guy in the company. Once the lights went out and the drill instructor left, we were left on our own, with the company petty officer. He was one of us, but he was elevated to the company petty officer. Then the cat calls would start at night, "Oh yes, I remember throwing the nigger into the swamp." I knew who was doing it so at night I would crawl out of my bunk, with my combat boots on, after it was good and dark, and I would crawl over to their bunk and beat the shit out of them.

Boom, boom, boom, three shots, and then I would crawl back to my bunk and get in bed. During the day if something happened, I would tell the guy to meet me in the bathroom after lights out, because lights were always on in the bathroom. Once the lights were out we would go in the bathroom, throw a few blows, no hard feelings. We would go back and get in our bunks.

That happened throughout boot camp. By the time boot camp was over, I had their respect. We may not have liked each other, but they knew they couldn't say whatever they wanted, and I wasn't going to let it go. That was one thing that was great about growing up in a big family, I knew how to fight. After boot camp was over, the entire company elected me honor man of the company.

I was a team player; I was out front as the guide-on. When we were in competition in boot camp, we got these little flags attached to the guide-on to show that we were experts in marching, experts in school, or experts in drills. We had company competitions and we were one of the top companies. In our fifth week they gave us rifles, but I didn't get a rifle because I was the guide-on. So whenever the company was doing right shoulder, left shoulder, all the different shoulder movements, present arms, order arms, if we were marching, I would be twirling the guide-on. The company commander used to come up to me while we were marching, and he'd say, "You think you're hot shit, right?" That was a big joke to me, because he enjoyed watching me. I enjoyed doing it, and he could see that I was really enjoying the marching.

As we neared graduation, the company commander called me into his office and asked me "How would you like to go to Washington?"

I said, "For what?"

He said "How would you like to be in the Honor Guard?"

I said, "What is that?"

He said, "Well I see how much enjoyment you get out of marching. It seems like you really enjoy it and you're very coordinated. They're looking for a good man, and you have to be a certain height. You've got to be coordinated, because it's not a big unit, but it's a specific unit. They do parades, all kinds of ceremonial things, and you'll go to the White House." At the time, I had planned on going to school for electronics at Great Lakes where all the schools were at the time.

So I said, "No officer, no, no. I want to go to school; I want to get a trade."

He said "No, no, you'll be able to come back. It's just for a year and a couple of months. Plus, it's in DC, you're going to be close to New York, and you will be able to go home every weekend."

I said, "Okay yeah, that sounds good." I had no idea what the honor guard was, other than what he told me.

He said, "How would you like that option?"

I said, "Yeah I'd like to do that, as long as I will be able to come back."

So he said, "Yeah, you'll be able to come back."

The next step was to go before the brigade commander, who was in charge of five companies. I walked into his office, stood at attention, saluted and he said, "Seaman apprentice, I understand your company commander has recommended that you go to Washington DC to be in the Honor Guard."

I said, "Yes," and I gave him a snappy salute.

He said, "Okay, left face," and I'd snap it, "right face," snapped that, "about face," I snapped that, "present arms," I saluted again. And he just said, "You're in, get out of here."

I said, "Aye, aye sir," and I did an about face and marched out of his office, and with that I was in the Honor Guard.

At graduation we were allowed to wear dress blues, standing on a field grinder, all the dignitaries and those families that could come were sitting in the grandstands. Then they had the navy band out there playing. The company commander was out front and when he called us to attention, I got a chill. "Company 372, attend hut!" We were snappy, and by that time we were all in shape.

Once I'd left boot camp, before I got to my next duty station, I had a thirty day leave. That was probably around November 25 or 26, 1962 and I went home for the first time in twelve weeks, and it was a joyous occasion. My dad met me, and took me home. I was in my dress blues, fresh out of boot camp.

My family was all at home and my friends came over. Unbeknown to me, the entire time that I was in boot camp, my brother Joe, who was a year older than I was, had worn all my clothes. All the clothes that I had made, all the clothes that I had bought in my senior year of high school, he was out having a fashion show standing on one of the main terraces in our neighborhood greeting everybody in the neighborhood. They called him the, "Mayor of East Elmhurst," and every day he would have on a different outfit that belonged to me.

Normally, if I had been home and that happened, I probably would have boxed his ears, but I think the thirteen weeks that I spent in boot camp matured me. I had grown, definitely physically, but also I had matured as a person, I was not so hot-tempered. Normally I would have been ready to fight, especially when it came to my clothes, because I had taken so much care in making them and in taking care of them. I'm like that to this day, really sensitive about my clothes. My dad took me shopping and bought me a couple of outfits. This time, because I was going to a duty station, I was going to take all my clothes that weren't ruined; I was going to take them back to DC with me.

Being home was a joyous occasion; my mom made my favorite meal which was chicken and sweet potato pies, which I love. She would always make maybe ten pies, but I would always get five because she knew how much I loved sweet potato pie; even to this day I'd kill for a sweet potato pie.

My big day, the Kennedy family followed us out of the cathedral.

Chapter Three

THE GUARD

It was a good thirty day leave and I even cut it short because I was very excited to get to Washington, to see what the future held for me. I stayed at home my twenty-five days and then I got on a greyhound bus at the port authority with my sea bag and my other gear and headed to Washington.

Oh, man! It was exciting because I had never been away – other than being in boot camp and being on that base or at Great Lakes. It was the first time that I had ever been on a base of any kind.

I remember getting to the port authority and having to jump in a cab and take the cab to the naval base and when I got to the gate, there were Navy guards at the gate. Part of the responsibility of the honor guard was to man the gates coming on to the base. The cab driver stopped at the gate and asked where he was supposed to go, and was told to go to the administration building, straight down the road. It was a building that they called the "Quarter Deck." It was the main entrance to the quarter deck, as it would be on a ship. When you walked up the ramp, the first place you would come to would be the quarter deck and that's the main area where the officer of the day would watch and everybody was located in that one area.

I walked into the main area and I had my sea bag and other little bags and I said, "I'm here, Hubert Clark, reporting for duty for the honor guard."

He said, "Okay, just go up those steps and you'll find the honor guard on the second deck."

I struggled with my bags getting up to the second deck and asked a guy, "So where do I report?" and he showed me to the office. I put my bags outside the office door and I went in, snapped to attention. His name was Lieutenant Simonitis, and he was the officer of the day, but he was also the executive officer of the honor guard. I went in, snapping to attention, giving him a salute and handed my orders to him and said, "Seaman Apprentice, Hubert Clark reporting for duty, sir."

I went at ease, gave him my papers and he said, "Welcome aboard," and he asked me where I was from, and how I got into the honor guard. I explained to him. Then he said, "How tall are you?"

I said, "5 feet, 11 inches."

He said "Pall bearer."

I said, "Excuse me sir, what is that?"

He said, "You're going to be a booty sniffer."

I said, "Booty sniffer?" I knew how that sounded, so I asked, "What is that?"

He said, "Okay, somebody will show you your bunk and you'll be able to put your stuff away." He explained the rules to me, and he said, "Stay squared away, and your APO, Acting Pay Officer, will talk to you. You're going to be in the first platoon."

I said, "Yes sir," snapped to attention, gave him a salute, turned around and came out of the office and met the first-class petty officer we used to call "Boats" He was the first petty officer, and he was in charge of the first platoon.

Boats was like an old salt. He had been in the Navy 23 years, but he was assigned to the army guard. As we were walking down to the dorm, I said, "Excuse me Boats, what's a booty sniffer?"

He said, "You're going to be carrying bodies."

I was always afraid of dead people, and when he said that, I said "What?"

He said, "You've got to be over six feet to be in a firing party, or the firing squad.

I thought to myself, if I had known that, I would have told the officers how I felt. So that's how I become the booty sniffer or a pallbearer. My first day there I got stowed away, put my uniforms up, and had my locker and key. Then Boats told me, "When you get stowed away, you should come to my room, and I will explain to you everything that you need to know, need to do."

I went to his room and he told me the rules. He gave me a booklet of the dos and don'ts. He gave me a brace; he gave me the colored brace that I wear on my belt, when I went out on detail.

We shined our brass with Brassos, and I burnished it and shined it. We had to get our shoes polished white and we had to get white that extra sole. We also had a horse shoe on the heel, and then we had cleats stuck on the front and on the side. So when we were marching heel to toe, it sounded like a horse. The sound was great when everybody marched in unison.

Everybody was assigned to a rifle. We had to take care of our rifles, cleaning it along with a bayonet. Those were used when we had a parade or any kind of detail.

We would train every day getting the difficult routines down. Unless we had a detail, we were up on the third deck, what we called our training area. We would train how to carry out military funerals. Since this was my first time I would go and I would watch how they trained. These guys were good. One would have to see it to really appreciate how they trained, how they carried out military funerals.

So for the first month, I did not have an opportunity to go out and carry out any funerals because I was still in training. When the first platoon had the detail for the day, I would go to Arlington, but the only ones there were pallbearers, the firing squad, and the person that was in charge of the team. If it was a Priest funeral, ten guys were part of the entourage. A chief was in charge of the pallbearers and the firing squad. The higher the rank, the bigger the funeral was. The biggest funeral would be called an 87. That would be a full naval military funeral with three platoons of enlisted men, the firing squad, and the officer in charge of the honor guard. He would be in charge of the entire ceremony.

My first funeral I was shaking in my boots. I was nervous although I knew what to do, but this was the first time that I had ever handled a casket along with the team. I remember we were sitting on the bus waiting for the hearse to show up. As soon as we spotted the hearse, we jumped out, and formed up. The firing party went twenty yards away from the graveside and when it formed up, I was sitting on the bus and I was saying to myself, "I know I can do this, I know I can do this." I was not at the head or the foot; instead I was more or less in the middle, where most of the new guys started out because the head and foot had more responsibility. Because I was new, they put me in the middle, so whatever mistakes I made could be covered up. I felt that I was ready. I remember I was the only one looking out of the window because I was nervous so I was the first one to spot the hearse. I was the first one off the bus while everybody else was taking their time because they knew what they were doing. I was excited because this was my first funeral. I was so cognizant that the entire time the remains were pulling up, I was practicing in my head – okay you do this, you follow, if they say three paces, you take the three paces with no turning, and if they say four paces forward, then you take the four paces forward and then you turn in. Three paces means we walk up three paces and stop. Three paces forward means we take three paces forward and turn in. We turn in because once the hearse passes you, depending upon if it is on the right or the left, we turn either to the right or the left towards the back of the hearse.

If the hearse pulled up, we would be right on top of it, since we are about four or five feet up from the hearse. We don't want the hearse to go by and hit us, so we back away. When the hearse pulls up, then the person in charge of the group would say, "Body bearers, three paces forward." So we would take three paces forward and then we go to parade rest. That means we had our back and then if we're not up to the hearse, he'll say, "Body bearers, two paces forward." Then we go up two paces and then we automatically turn in towards the door of the hearse. Now we're facing the back of the hearse and then he'd say, "Body bearers, two paces." Two paces would bring us right up to the door of the hearse and the person in charge would open the hearse – open the door and then we would start to pull the remains out. Everything is done at attention. Nobody is leaning over, because we want to maintain military precision. That's the whole purpose of a military funeral, to let this be the last respects for this man. Nothing is done haphazardly. When the casket comes out, we make sure that the flag is on right; we make sure that the foot of the casket always goes toward the gravesite first. The head of the casket is where the blue is. So when we're marching toward the graveside, we're taking side-steps to get away from the hearse and then the person in charge of the funeral or of the pall bearers would nod his head so we would start walking towards the gravesite. Once we get to the gravesite, the family is following and everybody's standing up. We had to be in shape because a lot of the times, when we would get to the gravesite, we wouldn't just drop the casket down, we had to slowly lower the casket.

Once we would get on the gravesite, we would side-step along boards would be on the gravesite and we would just half-step, or side-step onto the gravesite. Once we were all on the board, then we would slowly lower the casket onto the gravesite, onto that platform at the gravesite. Nobody would come up until we all had our hands on the flag and then we would all come up together with the flag in hand. And that's the way we would stay until we would get the nod from the funeral director. After Taps, after the firing party, then we would fold the flag, hand it to the funeral director who then would hand it to the family.

After the funeral ended, and the family left, we would pull the boards out from underneath the casket and the casket would slip down into the grave. We would never lower the casket while the family was at the gravesite because sometimes they would get emotional, throwing themselves on the casket.

After four months, I had lost any kind of fear about going out to Arlington. There were days when we would go out and we would have four or five funerals in one day. We'd just be jumping from section to section toward funerals. The military provided us with packed lunches, that we would eat on the bus. We would have half an hour, 45 minutes and then we would head on to the next funeral. There were days we'd be at the cemetery with six to seven funerals. We would have a funeral every 35 or 40 minutes.

I first set foot in Arlington National Cemetery in January 1963, and despite all the funerals I had participated in during that time, I never really gave death much thought. I was young and what young man thinks death is going to reach out for him? I never considered the possibility until November 22, 1963.

John and Jackie Kennedy in the Dallas motorcade November 22nd, 1963
Nellie Connally is in the foreground at left.

Chapter Four

THE LONGEST DAY

The morning of November 22, 1963, started with having reveille at 6:00 A.M. as usual. Since it was Friday, we didn't have any details that day. Guys would actively G.I. (clean up) the dorms. Everybody went up to the third deck, on the third floor, where we have the TV room. Then we also had the muster area and the practice area where we would normally practice funerals. We would have a mock set up of the casket on a grave site where we would normally be practicing our routines.

But for that day, Friday November 22nd, we didn't have any funerals or any other kind of details. So we all went up to the third deck where we would iron our uniforms and shine our shoes. It was just an area that everybody in the guard congregated to – when we didn't have any details. But on that particular day we were up there early, watching the news on TV and preparing to go home for Thanksgiving, because it was the holiday season,

Everyone that didn't have a duty was preparing to go home for the Thanksgiving holidays. As the morning proceeded and as we got close to the afternoon, they were showing the president in Dallas and what his itinerary was going to be that day. Suddenly, there was a news flash; breaking news that President Kennedy had been shot! At that point – everything just stopped. We were all glued to the TV, even the commander and other officers that were assigned to the guard came up to the third deck.

Everyone was stunned. At that time, we did not realize whether or not this was some kind of an attempt by a foreign government or somebody trying to do something to President Kennedy from a foreign country. We did not know whether he was dead or alive. The entire base went on alert, because that time was right after the Cuban missile crisis.

Everybody was uneasy, it seemed as though everything in the area, especially in the DC area, the weather just became overcast, as if there was a sense of doom.

We didn't realize or we didn't know at that time if the president had been mortally wounded, just that the president had been shot. But nobody understood whether it was a body wound or a head wound. There was just somebody shooting at the president's motorcade. I was in disbelief. Just like the rest of the guys and guards we were all young. I was probably one of the youngest in the guard.

From that point on, everybody just stopped whatever they were doing. The master room area was packed with the entire guard. Even people that worked in the administration building, were coming upstairs to look at the TV, because we had the only TV in the building

We were all glued to the TV. Every time the announcer or the broadcaster would say something, we were all hanging on. Was he okay? Was it serious? Were we going to war? Was it war? If so, with whom? The commander was up there, the executive was up there and all the other pay officers were up there. As time went on, we questioned, "Oh my god, what's going to happen next?

At 1:00 pm on November 22, 1963, the president was pronounced dead. Everybody knew that nobody was going anywhere. It was a tragedy that this had happened. Some guys were close to tears. We could hear it in their voices.

Walter Cronkite came on TV, and I think for anybody Walter Cronkite was the newsman's newsman. When we saw the way he broke down, guys were close to tears. We knew that we were going to play a part in what was going to take place next. We knew there was going to be a funeral, but we didn't know exactly what part we were going to participate in, other than being in the parade or in the ceremonies.

As the day went on, we were all upstairs. The commander and the exec went downstairs because the commander of the unit was getting calls from the military district of Washington that takes care of all big events in DC. Around 4:00 pm, my commander, Commander McNulty came over to the loud speaker and said, "Hugh, report to the guard office." I had no idea why I was being summoned.

When my name came over the PA system, I went down to the office and Commander McNulty said to me, "Hugh, you need to saddle up." He didn't say who but he said, "They will be here to pick you up." I didn't even ask who, what or why. I saluted him, turned and went back to my dorm area and made sure I started laying out my dress uniform, my white belt and all my brass. I started getting dressed.

I didn't know where I was going, but McNulty had said, "Saddle up and report back to the office." It took me maybe 15 minutes. There's a lot of preparation of white gloves, brass, and belts to make sure everything is just right. When I finished, I reported back to the guard office and McNulty told me, "Go wait down on the corner deck. Someone will be picking you up and you will be going to Andrews Air Force Base." I knew that Andrews Air Force Base was where Air Force One came and went.

I didn't ask what I would be doing, or who I should report to. McNulty said, "Follow their orders when you get there."

I don't want to say I was excited, but I was nervous because I had been to Andrews Air Force Base numerous times but never for something like this. I didn't know what part I would be playing. Would I be like an escort for dignitaries, a walk through or just be in place as part of a contingent to be present? I was down there for maybe 15 minutes and the snow patrol military police showed up. I got into the car and I said, "Where are we going?" The driver said, "Andrews Air Force Base."

When we left the base, there were no words exchanged. As we rode through DC, the streets were empty. For a Friday around Thanksgiving, this silence was unheard of. It was overcast. The sun had been out that day but now DC seemed like a ghost town. Once we arrived at Andrews Air Force Base, there were people all over the place, there were military police, men in suits, it was very crowded.

We pulled onto the base and drove up onto the tarmac, the airstrip. When I got out of the car, I saw Lieutenant Bird and I walked up to him and said, "Assuming Hugh Clark, Navy Honor Guard."

He said, "Okay, I want you to fall in with these guys." And it was James Felder, Richard Gaudreau, Bud Barnum, Tim Cheek and Doug Mayfield. I didn't know this at first, but I learned who these fellows were in the days that followed. We were all together. Lieutenant Bird was the officer in charge. Another set of pallbearers were stationed there also. Then Lieutenant Bird said to us, "This is what's going to happen. When the president's plane arrives, the elevated truck is going to back up, the first set of casket team members will remove the remains from Air Force One onto the elevated truck. Then this team will remove the casket and place it in the navy ambulance." That's how it was supposed to go.

Shortly thereafter, Air Force One came down the runway. It was maybe 20 yards from where we were standing when it stopped. The elevated truck backed up, the back door of the plane opened up, and we saw the first casket team on the truck. The elevated truck was raised and the team placed the casket on the elevated truck. As it was lowered, the navy ambulance was moved in place. We proceeded to remove the casket from the elevated truck and placed it in the ambulance.

There was no talking. Everything was done by a head nod. Once Lieutenant Bird had explained it to us, we knew what we were supposed to do.

As we moved to remove the casket off the truck, all hell broke loose. We had it three quarters off the truck, sliding it toward the end of the elevated truck. I was at the front of the casket when all of a sudden we were rushed by some civilians and General Godfrey McHugh. His exact words were, "This is my commander-in-chief." Bud Barnum was knocked out of the way. Gaudreau was almost knocked out of the way. The casket dipped because when these people rushed from both sides of the casket, I thought we were just supposed to let them have it.

When we let go, the casket dipped because they didn't know how to handle a casket. They did not know that the shifting weight of the casket was a quarter of the way onto the truck. Once we were pushed aside, there weren't enough of them to handle it. As the casket dipped, we were close enough to grab it and steady it and move it towards the ambulance. I was pulled aside, and they were able to push the remains into the navy ambulance.

At that time I looked up and I could see Jackie Kennedy, Bobby Kennedy and other dignitaries standing on the elevated truck. I remember thinking, "Oh my god, what is she going through?" Loading the casket lasted for at least a minute because it was done so haphazardly. No one's remains should have been treated like that, let alone the President of the United States. Once the casket was in the waiting ambulance, the door closed, and Jackie Kennedy was helped off the elevated truck. Lieutenant Bird formed us up again and I believe what he said to us was, "Oh my God."

Many hands tried to help with Kennedy's casket. As we were trying to take it off the lift, the casket was almost dropped due to interference, and I was almost crushed, caught between the casket and the gray Navy ambulance.

I think one of us might have said, "We almost dropped it." I know Lieutenant Bird was very disgusted at the way the casket had been handled. We formed up again on the side, and the ambulance, along with the dignitaries and the motorcade pulled off before President L.B. Johnson even had an opportunity to come down from Air Force One. Lieutenant Bird was getting instructions from Major General Philip Wehle, who was in charge of the Military District of Washington as to our next step. I heard Lieutenant Bird say, "This is the team that I want," and Major General Wehle said, "Okay, let's enter the helicopter."

We formed up, standing at attention, and we marched toward the army helicopter. General Wehle got in first, then Lieutenant Lipsey and then the rest of the casket team. Shortly thereafter we were airborne. Lieutenant Bird sat next to me, and General Wehle sat across from me. Lieutenant Bird commented to General Wehle that we almost dropped the casket because of the intrusion of all those people that didn't know what they were doing. General Wehle stated, "It won't happen again. It won't happen again."

Once we were airborne, I remember we shadowed the motorcade. I was excited and also frightened because I had never been on a helicopter before. I was looking out the windows, seeing the lights go by and saw the motorcade below us as we traveled from Andrews Air Force Base to the Bethesda Naval Hospital.

The helicopter ride lasted a good 25 to 30 minutes. It was already dark so we could see the lights of the motorcade. We were up high enough not to hit any telephone lines, but we weren't so high that we couldn't distinguish the motorcade itself.

Once we were near Bethesda Naval Hospital, we split off ahead and landed. I thought it was the helicopter landing area, but I couldn't really distinguish what it was because it was dark. There was a pickup truck waiting for us in the landing area. Lieutenant Bird put us in the back of this pickup truck. General Wehle and Lieutenant Lipsey got into an official vehicle. They went one way, and we went another way.

Once we got into the pickup truck, we went around the back of the hospital and came out on the right side of the hospital, the front of the hospital. We got out of the pickup truck and we formed on the right side of the main doors of the hospital. We were there for approximately 10 minutes when we saw the motorcade coming from our right side, up towards the front of the hospital. Once the motorcade and the navy ambulance went past us a little bit, we were supposed to move on to the ambulance to remove the casket. Just as the ambulance pulled up, we started to move on to the ambulance. It seemed as though there had to be maybe 100 photographers coming out of nowhere. Jackie Kennedy and Bobby Kennedy got out of the navy ambulance and went into the hospital. The photographers proceeded to rush the navy ambulance, at which point the navy ambulance took off. It just took off.

Right after that happened, we proceeded to move on to the ambulance. Lieutenant Bird's command was, "Back to the truck." We jumped back into the truck and started chasing the navy ambulance. We didn't have any points of reference in terms of the ambulance. All we knew was we were in the truck chasing this navy ambulance. We could see red lights. The driver had to know the grounds better than anyone else, so he just followed the ambulance. We might have gone around the hospital twice. At that point in time, Lieutenant Bird must have gotten the word because we went back to the hospital where the navy ambulance was waiting for us. We got out of the truck and we proceeded to remove the bronze casket. We proceeded up the ramp to the back of the hospital. With James Felder in front of me, Tim Cheek to his right, I was behind Felder. Bud Barnum was behind me, and we proceeded to guide the casket out of the ambulance and up to the ramp.

As we cleared the ambulance and started up the ramp, General McHugh pushed Bud out of the way grabbing the casket again. We had to maneuver in such a way because of the ramp itself. We were in between the two railings so we had to make a turn. On the first turn, we had to make a right to get up to the loading platform. We had to raise the casket, a little above the waist to clear the casket because we all couldn't fit between the railings. Once we got it up to the upper loading dock, someone opened the back door and there was a dolly waiting for us. We had to almost turn the casket on its side just to get it in the door because six of us couldn't fit through the door. It wasn't one of those double doors that we could carry the casket through. So we had to turn it on its side to get it through the door and place it on the dolly. Once we got it down on the dolly, again, there were three men on each side. Lieutenant Bird was in the back, and we wheeled it down the hall and into the anteroom where we were told, "Stop right here."

Once we delivered the casket, we walked back outside of the anteroom where we were placed on guard. I was on one side. Bird was on the other and then down the hall there was another set of doors, where Doug Mayfield and Timothy Cheek stood guard.

We must have gotten there around 8:00. I wasn't looking at my watch, I don't even think I had a watch on, but the official record said it was 8:00. We were standing outside the doors of the anteroom and there were six of us taking turns. I can remember seeing a man I later learned was the x-ray tech Jerrol Custer. I remember someone bringing food down because none of us had eaten. I remember trying to eat something

I remember Lieutenant Bird came out one time and asked us if we wanted to go in and look. I said "No." There was a point when we were inside the anteroom, that General McHugh came out and we asked him, "What's going on in there?" He was angry and he said, "I can't believe the way Johnson treated Mrs. Kennedy." He was very upset about what had happened. At the time, we didn't know what he was talking about.

I remember that Admiral Burkley came out one time and some of the guys asked him how it looked, or how bad the president was. He was explaining to them. I remember holding the morgue door open for him and looking for a good five to ten seconds, seeing the President's body lying on the table, and to me looking like he was sleeping. I could not see any wounds. I could not see any distinguishing things that would make me believe that he was hurt or that he had been shot. But I saw him only from the waist up because there was a sheet covering his lower extremities. I remember looking at his head because they said it was a head shot. I remember his neck; it looked like his neck or his head was on a block. It was a quick ten seconds and then I looked away and closed the door. From that point on, we were taking turns, two guys would sit down, and four guys would stand guard.

I don't recall how long we had to stand guard at the doors, but I don't think anybody was tired because everybody was so tensed up and the adrenaline was flowing. If they had told us that we had to stand up the whole night, we would have done it. We were told not to let any photographers or any unauthorized people come through the doors. We didn't know who was authorized and who wasn't authorized. We had guys in suits, and military generals and admirals going back and forth. We didn't know who belonged and who didn't belong. But anybody that had a camera, we held at bay.

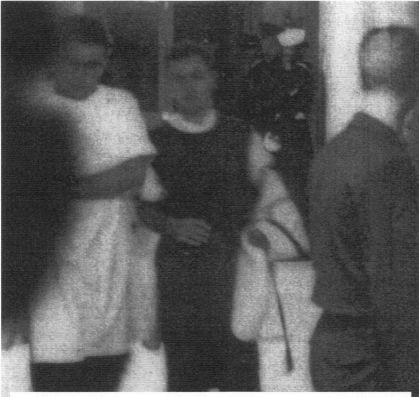

X-ray technician Jerrol Custer(left) and his assistant Ed Reed. I am in the background, guarding one of morgue doors.

One thing distinguishing the secret service, were that they all had pins on their lapels. Generals and admirals we knew because they were in uniform. The lead aprons identified the x-ray technicians. They belonged there. The guys with cameras were being kept back by somebody else. They weren't even allowed around the morgue area. We couldn't see the other people stationed in the area. We were the only guards around the morgue, just the six of us.

At no time did I see any other casket come through either one of those two doors to the morgue, other than the mahogany casket which was brought in around midnight.

We knew it was a different casket because Lieutenant Bird said that the other casket was banged up and so we were changing caskets. We could see the casket being brought in. Lieutenant Bird said that he was going to be placing this casket in the ambulance.

Once the President's body had finally been prepared for burial and was placed in the burial casket, it was around 4:00 in the morning. Lieutenant Bird made sure that there was a flag to drape over the casket. Then the casket was again brought into the anteroom. We removed the mahogany casket, placed it back into the navy ambulance, and we then got into a limousine rather than a helicopter.

Once we got into the limousine, we were right behind Jackie Kennedy, right behind the family, because we had to be in a position where we were able to get out and be formed up before the ambulance got to the White House. We had a police escort because we had to speed up to get there, get out of the motorcade and then speed up again.

We were really closing at a good pace. Everything was locked off on the motorcade group. People might think it's a little strange, but the entire time there was no conversation. We were all nervous; the adrenaline was flowing. We had been up since 6:00 the previous morning. We were running on fumes. There was no conversation until Lieutenant Bird told us what we were going to do and how we were going to do it.

The motorcade sped on ahead waiting for the ambulance to pull up under the overhang of the White House. We took the casket out of the navy ambulance and got it into the White House. Jackie Kennedy and the other dignitaries followed us down the hall towards the East Room. We had the casket on the dolly and we were holding it and guiding it down the hall towards the East Room of the White House. Once we got it into the East Room, we removed it from the dolly and we placed it on the catafalque. We stood guard over the casket. Jackie and Bobby Kennedy came in and we moved back from the casket and turned our backs so they could have their privacy. I think that's when they opened the casket.

Leaving the East Room at the White House taking President Kennedy's remains to the Capitol Rotunda.

Once they left the East Room we had to stay put until the Death Watch arrived. The Death Watch is a group of personnel from each branch of the service with an officer in charge who stands guard over the remains. They switch half an hour on, half an hour off. We were the first Death Watch because the other personnel hadn't been informed yet. So we had to stay near the remains for maybe 45 minutes before the Death Watch arrived and relieved us.

We went downstairs to the floor below to the main floor of the White House and men were sitting in chairs. I was lying on the floor. We were exhausted. We each had to wait for a ride back to our respective barracks. We all needed transportation back to the Armor Guard Barracks in Anacostia. I don't know how long we were there, but when I left the White House that morning it was daylight.

After I left the White House, I went back to the naval base where I had to get my uniforms ready and try to get some sleep. I slept maybe an hour or two before I had to refurbish my uniform and my shoes. I had been up all night. I don't even remember sleeping, between the excitement and the adrenaline. I don't even remember the guys at the base asking me any questions. I do remember that all the phones were turned off, with no calls coming in and no calls going out.

On Saturday we, the casket team, had to meet back at Arlington Cemetery. We also realized that two men had to be added because we were struggling with that casket, even with seven of us, because it was so heavy. We knew that the next day we were going to have to go up the Capitol steps to the rotunda. We met back at Arlington that evening at the Tomb of the Unknown Soldier, where we had another casket, an empty casket that was weighted to go up and down the Tomb of the Unknown Soldier steps.

We all knew this was going to be an ordeal because the Capitol steps are not wide. Going up and down one person is on the step at a time. So we had to take short steps to ensure that nobody stepped on anybody's heel and Lieutenant Bird wanted to make sure that we were comfortable doing it. He was the type of officer who made sure that we were prepared to fulfill the task so we went up and down those steps many times.

I remember the guard at the Tomb of the Unknown Soldier steps saying, "Down on the head, up on the foot," to make sure that we had the casket leveled. We were the only people in Arlington Cemetery at that hour. The gates were closed and nobody else was going around the sections. I remember thinking, "Isn't this something, that at night, at the Tomb of the Unknown Soldier steps we're practicing to make sure we get this right."

On Sunday we went back to the White House where we removed the remains. I remember we marched from the White House to the Capitol rotunda while the family followed behind. I remember Jackie Kennedy,

Bobby Kennedy, Ted Kennedy, all the dignitaries went from the White House to the Capitol rotunda behind the remains. That entire Sunday the President lay in state at the Capitol.

After we had placed the President's body at the Capitol, we went back to the Tomb of the Unknown Soldier and practiced for hours and hours, going up and down the steps.

Sunday night I tried to get some rest and made sure everything was squared away. Shoes, vest, hats, uniforms, just making sure everything was in proper order. I wanted to talk to my family, but nobody was calling in, nobody was calling out. All the phones were off the hook. None of us had the opportunity to call out or receive calls.

On Monday, November 25, 1963, we made sure everything was in order, because we knew it was going to be a long day. We were going to have to go to the Capitol, bring the remains down, and then go to St. Mathew's Cathedral. We marched both beside the caisson and behind the caisson. Then from St. Mathew's Cathedral we had to march to Arlington National Cemetery, a very long walk.

At the top of the Capitol steps, we were standing and holding the casket. I thought, "I hope we don't have to stand here long because it's going to be a struggle getting down these steps." I could feel the weight of that casket. We were breathing hard going down; we were straining.

We were more afraid going down, hoping to God that we had practiced enough, that we knew we would take one step at a time. When a man left that step, I would be on that step to make sure I didn't miss because going down was more dangerous than going up.

We were not afraid of dropping the casket. I think for all of us, the inner strength of all of us, were working as a team. Everything that we had learned prior to this funeral, the other funerals that we had done, and Lieutenant Bird being patient with us, making us practice, making sure that we had it down to a "t" paid off in the end. Once we got the casket down the steps, we had to be close, but could hear almost a sigh of relief. Then we had to raise the casket up and we could not bend over or squat down a little bit and push it up. Everybody at the same time had to lift as one person and raise it up and then slide it onto the caisson.

Once it was on the caisson, we tied it down and made sure that the flag wouldn't blow off. Then we formed up and all the other servicemen lined up. Then we started for St. Mathew's Cathedral, another walk.

In my peripheral vision, I had never seen so many people on the streets of Washington, DC. As I moved up the street, I could see the enormity of the crowd which had to be 10 or 12 feet deep. It was amazing. I'm sure people had driven from all over the United States to be in DC for the funeral. I could hear people above the drum beat and then I heard the rest of the band kick in with the death march. I couldn't hear anybody yelling out but I could hear people sobbing. They were literally crying as we marched by them.

For me it was all about the people of DC. I wasn't thinking about the entire world watching. The crowds were massive from what I could see peripherally, and as we marched the music was very solemn. Once we arrived at St Mathews Cathedral, the other services, the military, had performed. Then we came alongside of the caisson, and we unbuckled the straps across the casket, across the flag.

Then once the music started, *Hail to the Chief,* we began to slide the casket off of the caisson. Once we got it off the caisson, we turned and started heading into St. Mathew's Cathedral where Cardinal Cushing met us on the street level where he blessed the casket. Then we moved up the steps and into the foyer area of St. Mathew's Cathedral. From what I could see St. Mathew's Cathedral looked beautiful from the doorway. Then Sergeant Felder and I wheeled the casket down the center aisle to place it in front of the altar.

Once we placed the casket on the altar, we turned it sideways. James Felder and I left the altar area and walked back out to the foyer where we waited for the mass. Once the doors opened again, after the mass was over, we went back down to the altar, and we had to turn the casket so it would come out feet first.

As we went down and turned the casket, Cardinal Cushing came with the incense. He was blessing the casket again, and the incense went right

Carrying the president to his final resting place at Arlington National Cemetery.

up my nose. Tears came pouring down my cheek. I wasn't crying but the incense had gotten up my nose and tears started coming down. I heard a lady say, "Look, the sailor is crying."

But I never smiled or frowned, I just let the tears roll down my cheeks and then we started out slowly down the center aisle. When we got to the foyer area we all turned in, making sure that the flag was straight. We proceeded out of the St. Mathew's Cathedral, as the band played *Hail to the Chief.* We came down the steps and were standing there holding the casket, which never got any lighter. Once we came down the steps, Cardinal Cushing blessed the remains again.

Then we walked over to the caisson, turned in, raised the casket up, and slid it back onto the caisson, put the straps on, made sure that the flag was secure so wind wouldn't blow the flag. We then lined up alongside the caisson. We waited until the family got into their motorcade. We started out for Arlington National Cemetery and from that point we didn't realize how long or how far. The only thing we could hear was that drum beat. Then the rest of the band came in while we're marching and the entire time we just saw this mass of people all the way to Arlington.

I hadn't realized how far I had walked, but I knew that once we got to the Memorial Bridge, which I had crossed many times, that we were close because the Memorial Bridge is right outside of Arlington.

As we marched up, we saw men dressed in the red and white uniforms of the old Revolutionary Guard. It was just beautiful. We were alongside the caisson and when the caisson slowed down, we had to march in place until it started up again. Then we moved forward, four men on each side, Lieutenant Bird behind the caisson, and we beside it.

As we proceeded over the Memorial Bridge, we made a right and marched up into Arlington National Cemetery through the gates on the right side. We went around and followed the road around until we got up to the Robert E. Lee mansion.

Once the caisson stopped, we backed off as the caisson pulled up a little in front. Then we turned inward, ready to take the remains off the caisson. Once we did that we turned upward and started the long trek up to the gravesite after Cardinal Cushing blessed the casket first.

At the point the weight of the 1,300 pound casket became apparent because Cardinal Cushing and other pastors were assisting him, were moving very slowly. At one point we bumped them with the casket because we were on slippery ornamental roads around the grave site. We were trying to maintain our footing but they were moving so slowly that we felt as if we were standing still. Then when they got bumped with the casket, they sped up a little bit.

Once we got up to the gravesite, we had to put the casket down. We had to bend over because we couldn't stand up straight, because the gravesite had to be wide enough. The platform for the remains was the only thing that I really thought about, as heavy as that casket was. "I hope when we set it down that it just doesn't drop right down." The casket is never lowered while the family is at the gravesite.

At the gravesite, we placed the President's casket on the boards across the gravesite. Before we came back up we made sure we gripped the flag, so the flag comes up at the same time, taut, never sagging. We stood there in the cold throughout the gravesite service with our white gloves holding the brand new flag.

My fingers were cramping up from all the marching from St Mathew's to Arlington. I was starting to get a little cramp in my lower muscles, but I was standing there at attention holding on to that flag, looking straight ahead into the eyes of the person in front of me,

We folded the flag, in one of the best flag folding ceremonies in which I have ever or will ever participate in. Nothing showed but that blue fold. Once it was handed over to the funeral director, he handed it to Jackie Kennedy. We couldn't see that, but that's the procedure, because we were looking straight ahead. One thing that I remember about the gravesite is Cardinal Cushing blessing the casket as he spoke in Latin in his unique voice while everybody listened.

After the ceremony was over the family left the gravesite. We were still standing at the gravesite after all the dignitaries and everybody had left. Then The Black Knights from Ireland performed their silent drill. Through all of the ceremony we were standing there holding the flag, holding it taut. After all was done, we folded the flag. Then Mrs. Kennedy lit the eternal flame. Everybody left the gravesite and we, the Honor Guard, were the only ones standing there. We then did something unique. Lieutenant Bird marched us maybe five paces off the main gravesite. Then he had us salute. We were facing the casket or the remains and he said, "Present arms." We gave our final salute as the casket team to the Commander in Chief. That was the last funeral I participated in at Arlington National Cemetery, the burial of President John F. Kennedy.

I received a medal for my participation in JFK's funeral I'm getting ready to salute. I was in Italy at the time this picture was taken.

Chapter Five

HOMECOMING AND
MY NEXT JOURNEY

The morning after we laid President Kennedy to rest, I was on a bus from the Port Authority in Downtown Washington on my way back home. I had finished my tour of duty in the Navy Honor Guard and I had an opportunity to reflect back on the past four days during this four hour trip. Between sleeping and waking up on the bus, I was remorseful because I didn't have an opportunity to say goodbye to everyone. Once the funeral was over, we were so tired, Smitty[1] and I went back and got some much needed sleep. Before we realized it, reveille was going off at 6:00 A.M. and we knew we had to be out.

Alone I think things started to sink in, in terms of what I had just gone through. I was feeling very proud that my last funeral just happened to be the President of the United States. It was a feeling of really doing something great for the country and for my family, but again I didn't realize the magnitude at the time. It was just a matter of doing a good job for the Navy and for the country, but also to make my family proud. I think that the biggest thing for me was wondering how my family would react when I told them what I had done, not realizing that they had seen me on TV, because I never had an opportunity to speak to them.

When I got home I was treated as if l I had just won World War II. My friends, my family, my whole community were out there to greet. From the time that I came home my life was non-stop, going here and going there.

My dad was one of the proudest fathers in the world. He let me know because we stopped at every school I had ever attended, from the one in Patterson, New Jersey, PS 62, Mamaroneck Avenue to Mamaroneck Junior High, to my high school of fashion industry. The school hosted a special assembly for me. Then my dad took me to the Bible College where I spoke.

Life was so busy and I became so exhausted that I spent the rest of my leave in St. Albans Naval Hospital. I had a bad case of strep throat. My throat had almost closed up and between the Penicillin shots every four hours to at least being able to swallow something, my life was touch and go for a while back then.

---

1   Larry Smith was one of the two other Honor Guard members who were added to help carry the burial casket to Arlington because of the weight.

The following day after I got out of the hospital, I had to report down to Charleston, South Carolina Naval Base to catch a ship to go overseas. I flew out of La Guardia Airport down to Charleston along with three other men that had been stationed in Washington. Although they were not in the Honor Guard, we knew each other because we were all on the same base.

One of the men, Mugsy, was from Philadelphia. We had taken a cab from the airport to the main strip right outside the naval base when one of the men said, "Hey come on. Let's stop and have a beer before we check in." It was 1963. Everybody agreed to stop and have a beer, at the closest bar to the main gate. "We'll stop and have a beer and then we'll check in, get our sea bags; our big duffel bags with all our clothes in it."

So we went into the bar and Mugsy ordered four beers. The bartender brought back three and set them in front of the three white men. I was the only black military man. So Mugsy pushed his beer down to me because I was closest to the door. I picked it up and started to drink it when the bartender slapped it out of my hand. I said, "What'd you do that for?"

He said, "We don't serve niggers in here." That was the first time I had ever heard that expression. I really didn't understand what he was saying, but Mugsy did. Mugsy punched him and I thought, "Oh shit, it must be something bad."

We started fighting in the bar and other people joined in including civilians. It was us four against the bar. It seemed we were fighting a half an hour before we heard the sirens in the background. Somebody had called the police. We grabbed our sea bags and we were about 30 yards or 40 yards from the main gate.

We were running for the main gate because we knew if we could get on the base, the civilian authority couldn't come on the base and the base would not give us up. Once we got on the base, the state police pulled up to the main gate where we were all sitting on our sea bags.

We were out of breath just panting, sweating with our uniforms all disheveled. The Marines on the gate wouldn't let the civilian cops come on the base.

The State Trooper walked up to the gate and he pointed at me and said "Boy, don't ever let us catch you off this base because your momma will never see you again." It was at that time that I really felt, "Why am I fighting for this country and I can't even have a beer? I just buried the President of the United States and I cannot have a beer." If there was one time where I hated being in the military, this was that one time. It made me think of the Emmett Till case and tears just started running down my cheek. I think that was one of the most devastating and angry moments that I ever felt being in the military.

I remember checking in aboard ship. That was the first time that I had an opportunity to call home and speak to my father and talk to him and tell him what had happened. Being a pastor he said, "Your mom, your brothers and sisters and I are praying for your safe return." That made me feel better, but when my family was in New York and I was in the deep South, anything can happen.

I was stationed at Charleston, South Carolina, maybe a month before the ship took off and we started out for overseas. The first spot we hit was Naples, Italy, a new world experience. It seemed as though the people over in Europe accepted me more than the people in my own country.

I spent the rest of my tour of duty overseas. When it was time to come back home, I was having such a good time over there that I almost re-enlisted. The only reason I did not re-enlist was that all my friends back home were writing me, telling me how much fun they were having and wanting me to come home. They had a whole lot of things planned that we were going to do. That's what stopped me from re-enlisting and low and behold in August of 1966, I got discharged and returned to Charleston, South Carolina. I had matured and things didn't affect me as they had when I initially went south in 1963.

My attitude about the south had matured because I had grown as a person emotionally and physically. I had seen a lot overseas; I had heard a lot overseas. So when I came back life was a little different because the Civil Rights had been passed; the Voting Rights had been passed. It was a different time. It was maybe 13 days before I was discharged and I was on a plane, coming home, coming back to New York. I remember that on my first night home my mom had cooked my favorite sweet potato pie, chicken, potato salad and collard greens. She had all my favorite dishes so it was a day to remember!

When I came home, I had an opportunity to take it easy. My best friend and I went on a road trip for three weeks in his dad's blue Ford Fairlane convertible. We started in Baltimore, we went through Morgan State University first, and we partied there. Then we stopped and saw our friends who were going to the school. Then we went back in the car, went back to D.C. to Howard University and partied with our friends there. Then from Howard we went down to Campton, Virginia; then from Campton we went to North Upstate, partying with our friends.

For three weeks, we just partied having a house party every night. I just figured I was all for that because I had been in the military. I was mature, and I knew how to talk to women. That was a big thing. I had a head start on the college kids because I had been around the world and when they introduced me they would say, "Oh this is Hugh, this is Hubie, and by the way, do you remember President's Kennedy's funeral? Well this is the guy that was carrying his casket." That was always a conversational piece, especially with the pretty women. After the trip was over, I returned to New York and I had already taken the Police Exam but the class hadn't started yet.

Hugh working undercover narcotics on the streets of New York, 1968.

Chapter Six

STARTING A NEW CAREER

After I left the military and after some thought, I decided to become a cop. It was a civil service job that would include a good pension and benefits if I was thinking about getting married. It was a new career. I had never gone back to Great Lakes to finish electronics school. I didn't really have a trade and after being in the military, my interest in being a tailor or designer was gone. I had a couple of friends that were cops in the neighborhood, and I started talking to them about their profession. They sold me on it, but before the class had even started I decided to take a job at the UN, for the General Assembly.

I found out the UN was looking for investigators, so I went in and applied and was hired as an investigator. I met a lot of dignitaries, sitting in at the Security Council. My eyes were opened to different cultures coming together. Diplomats would argue fiercely, in the Security Council or in one of the other meetings, but as soon as it was over they walked out hugging each other, and shaking hands. I got to know some of them who invited me to parties around Christmas time. I was invited to some of the parties that they had at the UN and being able to take a girlfriend with me to the party was very impressive to women.

With pictures of the President's funeral hanging on the walls and with all the dignitaries that were there, I was able to point out, "That was me in the Navy." That became a conversational piece. Whenever they introduced me at a party, whenever we went to an Embassy party, every time somebody new came in they announced, "This is Ambassador so and so from" – and then they announced me as Officer Clark, US Navy who was President John F. Kennedy's Pallbearer. It was really a good experience for me.

Being an honor guard at JFK's funeral opened a lot of doors for me. Whenever my friends introduced me, they would always say, "Oh, this is my friend Hugh or Hubert or Hubie, he was in the military and oh, by the way he was one of President Kennedy's honor guardsmen."

People would say, "You're kidding, really?" It started a whole conversation with people. Even to this day, people that know me when I'm introduced to someone always say, "This is Hugh, he lives down by the garden and by the way you know he was..." and again it starts a whole conversation. Even people who did not support the President politically say, "Oh, you're in the history book," or "Man, you're in history" and I never looked at it that way.

After my time with the general assembly was over, I was asked to stay on and become permanent. It was just a three month job. I didn't have any intention of staying on because the job confined me. The UN wasn't what I wanted to do.

So I passed the police exam and joined the NYPD. I had just entered the police academy, when one of my instructors, Sergeant Baumet, started talking about all the jobs that the New York City Police Department did and didn't do at the time and what they were involved in as far as heads of State that came into New York and what he had done as a police officer. He chose to talk about the Kennedy funeral. He told how a contingent of New York City Police Department policemen were shipped down to Washington DC because many dignitaries had come into town and the police wanted to ensure they had tight security. I raised my hand, "I was there also, as a matter of fact I have pictures of the funeral." I said, "When I go home, I'm going to look and see if I can find you in any of the pictures." That night after school I went home and I found him in one of the pictures. The next day I made a copy for him. I took the picture to the academy and said "Sarge, I have a surprise for you." I showed him the picture. He freaked out. He was probably one of the happiest cops I'd ever seen. He ran over to the Police Academy and showed that photograph to everybody. As a result of that picture, he took a special liking to me.

Having him as a friend, gave me a bit of an edge. When you're in the academy, you need all the edge you can get. As we walked around in our uniforms people were scared to death because they thought you were going to pull out your gun and shoot them. Because we didn't have the training we were probably more frightened than they were. In New York when you're a rookie you wear different uniforms so that you are very distinguishable between the regular cops and rookie cops.

Whenever the rookies went out on the street a seasoned cop would be with them. Back then, a lot of demonstrations were going on so sometimes rookie police were out in the street by themselves. We were not to pull our guns out; they gave us a lot of don'ts and not a lot of do's.

I had been in the military and I was used to discipline. I knew how to carry myself, and I had handled weapons before. So this wasn't scary for me. I actually grew up in the street; I wasn't a guy that stayed in the house. I knew the city. I knew all five boroughs, I knew how to travel. So this wasn't a scary time for me. But it was scary for guys who came in from Rhode Island or from Worcester or from one of the outer boroughs.

Once I completed the academy, I got assigned to my first home precinct, a place called Fort Apache, the Bronx – the 41. Up in the Bronx on Simpson Street, it was one of the worst precincts in the city. It was wintertime, but we had not been cops long enough to get our overcoats. I remember my first shift was on Southern Boulevard in the Bronx, it was a midnight-to-eight shift.

Buildings were burned out, it was high crime area. The only thing that saved me that one night was the cold. There were not many people out on the street on the midnight-to-eight shift. I remember standing on the corner, right outside of a Western Union. I went in that Western Union every ten minutes to warm up. I would stand in there and the Western Union guy would say, "Come on in. There's a cot in the back. All of the guys come in here and take a nap." I said, "Really?"

Then he said, "Yes, the Sergeant knows." I remember I was in there trying to get warm and the Sergeant came by to sign my book but I wasn't out there. Every hour, the supervisor came by to sign the book asking, "Is everything okay? Do you have anything to report? Is anything suspicious?" Just to make sure that everything was okay on the posts.

I was inside getting warm because I didn't have an overcoat. It was probably 19 degrees, and that wind was whipping up and down Southern Boulevard so I went into that Western Union where it was nice and warm.

I went in, got warm, had a cup of coffee, talked to the guy for a few minutes, and went back outside. Then here came the Sergeant. He cracked his window about two inches, and said, "Where were you?"

I said, "Sir, I was inside getting warm. I was freezing."

The sergeant looked at me and said, "When I come by, I want to see you out here."

When I got back to the precinct, I was frozen stiff, and I asked the precinct captain, "Can I go on vacation?" I had friends that were cops in the neighborhood who talked me into wanting to be a cop. When I walked into the precinct after my shift was over and I asked him about vacation, he said, "What's your name?"

I said, "Hubert Clark."

He said, "Hey, you have been transferred."

I said, "What?"

The captain said, "Yes, you've been transferred to undercover." That was probably one of the happiest days of my life!

I had been a beat cop for exactly one night. The guys who had talked me into being a cop pulled strings and got me transferred. They knew I was good. They knew I'd been in the military. They knew my background. We were in this unit because I always showed them to be equals. They had submitted my name for the unit. That first night I thought to myself, "Whoa. Thank you Jesus for that." My friends had been the answer.

I went on vacation for a week and then I reported to my new unit – the Secret Detectives Special Unit.

The unit was comprised of street guys, with Afros and beards. We were all cops, but we looked young back then. The purpose of the unit was to infiltrate subversive organizations and gather intelligence. Then we would take it back to the office and submit it for the officers or the bosses to evaluate, to determine what was going on in the city as far as subversive organizations. Back then there were the SDS, Students for a Democratic Society, the Weathermen, the Black Panthers, the Black Liberation Army, and many subversive organizations that were rebelling against the establishment.

Our job everyday was to ride in unmarked cars. These cars could be gypsy cabs or other trucks or vans. We would disperse throughout the city where there was subversive activity taking place: Washington Square Park, Bryant Park, the village area, and all of the five boroughs. Every day we would go out gather this intelligence, write it down, keep daily records and take it back to headquarters. It would be evaluated and determined where the next hot-spot would be, where the next demonstration would be. These weren't just Black or White radicals, they were any radical, even if it was mixed. Out on the West Coast there was the Symbionese Liberation Army.

Those were the types of organizations that we would try to infiltrate to gather intelligence. Sometimes we were in deep cover, not just undercover but deep cover. We had Afros and beards, and we tried to fit into that environment. That's what the chief of detective special unit was like. We didn't go out to make an arrest. We went out to gather intelligence. I stayed there for three years until I got drafted into undercover narcotics.

I wanted to go into the undercover narcotics unit, because those were all intelligence units, anything not to go back to uniform. Because uniform was almost like a bulls-eye. Back then a lot of the subversive organizations were really radical and didn't have any problems killing cops.

My memories of working undercover narcotics are vivid. We were working Manhattan South and my partner and I were out making buys. Our jobs were to go out and make buys from people selling drugs. We would go out and we would make a buy. We would buy on Monday, buy on Tuesday, and we would lay off and do paperwork on Wednesday. Then on Thursday and Friday, we would get in our car and go out looking for the people we had bought from. We would have a walkie-talkie in the car and we had the back-up team that was working in the street with us. We never went out without a backup team in case something happened.

One of the many interesting cases we were working on was in the Manhattan South district, down on Rutledge and Stanton Street. My partner, whose street name was Caesar, went into this door down in Manhattan around Rutledge Street where the guy was telling him, "Hey, come on in. We're selling heroin inside this door." Back then the addicts used to take all the copper off the doors and the plumbing to sell to get drug money. My partner went into this house on Rutledge Street but it was a set up, and he didn't realize that when he went in. Three more guys were inside looking to take him out. The guy said to him, "Under the steps, go under the steps," and he went back there and made his buy, or what he believed to be his buy. They pulled a knife on him. Undercover agents do not carry an ID card or shield, instead they tuck it inside their pants. If drug dealers are patting the agent down, they are not going to find his shield. Caesar had left his ID card in his wallet. They had him up against the wall and I was outside up the block, waiting for him to come out when all of a sudden we heard all this gunfire. They tried to rip him off and started to stab him but he spun the guy that was trying to stab him and at the same time pulled his gun out and started firing. Since the dealers used to take all the door knobs off the doors, when they were trying to get out of the door, everybody was trying to get their fingers in the little holes for the knob and he was just firing away!

When we heard the gunshots, we came running back towards the building when we saw these four guys running down the block. My partner came out and I said, "What happened?"

He said, "They tried to rip me off."

I said, "You didn't hit anybody." Three-quarters away down the block, three guys dropped dead and one guy was paralyzed. So he had hit all of them.

Another time we got into a gun fight up on Southern Boulevard and Hoe Avenue where a guy tried to rip me off. The back-up team came when they saw me running with my gun out chasing this guy. They came and pursued the guy while I was maybe 20 feet behind him. When he turned around to fire, I was getting ready to shoot when a civilian came walking by. Just as the civilian got between us, I pulled up my gun and my bullet hit the wall where the guy's head had been. Initially I said, "Oh my God," because I thought I almost hit the civilian. The guy went down underneath the building. I never saw this guy touch the fence that was 15 feet up. He went over that fence and got away. I think if I had not pulled up, I would have shot the civilian in the head.

When I left narcotics after three years, I received my gold shield, my detective shield, and I went to the 83 squad. I became a precinct detective. The 83 squad was located on Wilson and Dekalb. Now as detectives, we investigated rapes, homicides, burglaries, anything that lead you to the investigation. Any type of investigative duties, we did. That's where I learned how to be an investigator.

I stayed with the NYPD for 22 years. I returned to college because I wanted to do something a little safer, as I got older and I wanted to help people in a different way. Unlike a lot of my fellow police detectives, what I saw on the street, the shooting and the drug deals had not changed my feeling on humanity.

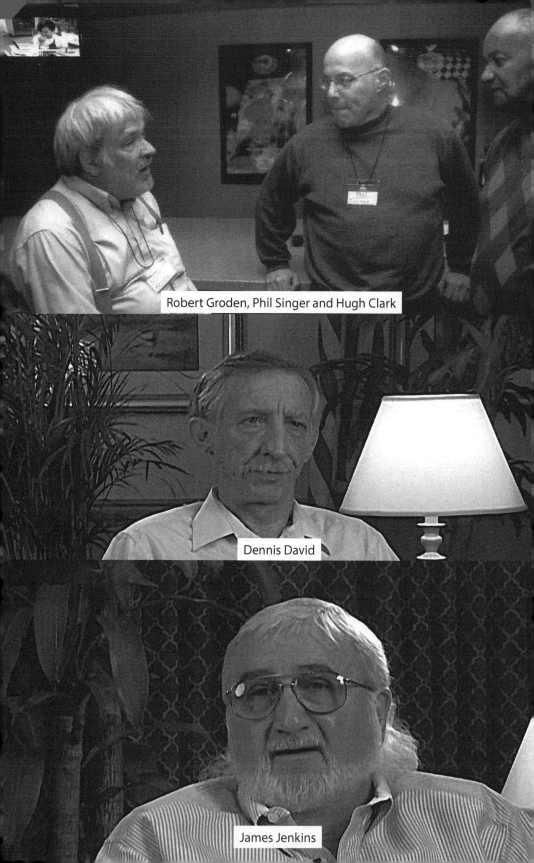

Robert Groden, Phil Singer and Hugh Clark

Dennis David

James Jenkins

Chapter Seven

THE EVENT AT WESTMONT

I retired in 2008 after being a drug and alcohol counselor and administrator for many years. My daughter graduated from the University of Florida and then moved to Atlanta, Georgia. Both my wife and I wanted to be near our only child, and after retiring, we decided to make the move to Atlanta. It's a move my wife and I have never regretted. The people are friendly, the heat has been good for my old bones, and I have plenty of time for my passion of golf.

My memories of my time in the Navy where I, with the help of my comrades, laid to rest the 35th President of the United States, my time as a New York detective, and my time as a drug and alcohol counselor seemed very far away. Occasionally, on an anniversary of President Kennedy's assassination, I would get a call from a newspaper reporter or someone wanting me to do a radio interview about my experiences on that tragic weekend of November 22, 1963. I would sometimes acquiesce to their requests. Always, there were the many letters with the request for me to autograph a picture of me with the rest of the honor guard carrying Kennedy's casket to Arlington National Cemetery.

I knew I had a small place in history because I was involved in John F. Kennedy's funeral. It had opened doors for me over the years, and at the very least, it made me the center of attention at cocktail parties, I felt I had been a small cog in the wheel in the history of that event – really just doing the job my country had required of me, as hundreds of people had done on that sad weekend so long ago.

In the winter of 2014, I received a phone call which would lead to a change in my understanding of John Kennedy's assassination and my role in its aftermath. A call that would make me question whether I and the others that carried the display casket into the morgue at Bethesda, Maryland, were used in the orchestration of a ruse – a ruse to leave a fake version of history, in essence, a lie that has persisted for 53 years.

String theory suggests that time is a fluid thing. It can flow forwards or backwards. I don't know if that's really true, but when I received a call from a man named Phil Singer in 2014, I felt as if I had been dragged back 5 decades in time. Phil introduced himself as a "truth seeker" in the assassination of JFK. He told me he had been a member of Mark Lane's citizen's commission of inquiry, when he was a teenager. (I had no idea

who Mark Lane was at the time, but doing my own research, now I do.)
Singer said he had tracked me down through the Internet, and with some
research, had found my phone number. He wanted to know what I remembered the night my fellow servicemen and I had carried Kennedy's
casket into the morgue at Bethesda.

I told Phil about meeting Air Force One at Andrews Air Force Base,
helping to unload the casket off the lift at the door of the plane, putting
it in the ambulance, the ride in the helicopter, shadowing the motorcade,
arriving at Bethesda, Maryland, a good 15 minutes before the motorcade
itself arrived, being told by Lieutenant Bird to get into the back of a pickup truck after the ambulance took off at a fast rate, how we tried to follow
it but lost it in the cold darkness of the night. Phil seemed quite interested
in that part of my memories, saying "So you lost the ambulance?"

At first I told him "No we didn't lose it – we just had to try to find it by
going around the complex two or three times."

Phil laughed at my explanation and said, "You sure you didn't lose the
ambulance?"

I returned Phil's laughter and admitted "Yeah, I guess you could say
we lost the ambulance."

I continued to tell Phil Singer the rest – about finally connecting with
the ambulance at the back of the morgue, taking the casket out of the
ambulance and taking it in to the hallway and perhaps into the Bethesda
morgue itself. I wasn't sure. I couldn't remember at that time and then
I told Singer about having to guard the doors to the morgue. I casually mentioned that while opening the morgue door for Dr. Berkley, I was
able to see inside the morgue and saw President Kennedy's body on the
morgue table. The lower half of Kennedy's body was covered by a sheet.
"Kennedy looked like he was sleeping, except his neck had some sort of
block under it making his chest lift up a little."

Phil said "Oh, okay."

I then told Phil, "I didn't want to see anymore, so I turned around and
continued to take my shift guarding the door."

Singer wanted to hear the whole tale, the night at the morgue, the next
day's events, preparing ourselves to carry the very heavy casket Kennedy
was to be buried in, my practicing at night going up and down the steps
at the Tomb of the Unknown Soldier with a weighted casket in order to
get the feel for what we would have to do while carrying Kennedy's casket
up the church steps for his memorial, and, of course, carrying his casket
up and down the Capitol steps and the long walk to Arlington National
Cemetery. I did my best to tell him all he wanted to know.

Then Phil Singer surprised me by saying, "I have a friend who is a
writer and filmmaker; his name is William Law and we are thinking about

bringing people that were involved in President Kennedy's autopsy together. We were thinking that if we could find the other members of Kennedy's honor guard we would invite all of you to come together for a reunion of sorts. We would record the event on film, for history, and it would be something you could pass down to your families. Would you be interested?" I had to wait about two seconds before I answered Phil with a "yes." The thought of seeing some of the men I had met so long ago and had been part of history with appealed to me and I thought it really would be something to participate in if the event was going to be filmed for history – and it would, of course, be something to pass onto my family. Singer told me I was the first of the honor guard members he had contacted. We agreed we would both try to locate the other members and see what we could come up with.

Over a period of weeks, Phil and I were both able to find and talk to almost all of the rest of the surviving members of the Kennedy casket team. The plan was to set a date that would be compatible for everyone. We were able to contact Tim Cheek in Florida, James Felder in South Carolina and Doug Mayfield and Bud Barnum in California. We unfortunately were not able to find Richard Gaudreau. I knew that Lieutenant Commander Bird had passed away years before due to injuries he sustained while serving in Vietnam. I was to find, with great sadness that Larry Smith and Jerry Diamond, the two men that were added later to the casket team to help with the events at the Kennedy funeral due to the sheer weight of the barrel casket, had also passed away in the intervening years.

It had been decided that the event where we would all get together for the film project would be held in Chicago in the suburb of Westmont. Unfortunately, as the event was being scheduled, Bud Barnum had another commitment and couldn't attend and Doug Mayfield had to bow out for health reasons. I was disappointed that all of the guys from the honor guard would not be able to attend the meeting in Chicago. But still, there would be Tim Cheek and James Felder and something that really intrigued me, the promise that some of the guys that had been inside the morgue helping with Kennedy's autopsy would also be there. Richard Lipsey, with whom Phil had been in contact over a period of several months, had said he might come, but his attendance was up in the air. As it turned out, Lipsey did show up for part of the Chicago event, and I must say his participation turned out to be rather bizarre.

Finally, Phil Singer and William Law set the date. We would all meet in Westmont, Illinois, on February 2nd, 3rd and 4th, 2015. I grew more and more excited as the days passed, getting closer to seeing men I had not seen in fifty-one years. When the day finally arrived, I was packed and ready. I made sure I packed warm clothes as the weather report said that

Chicago was going to be cold. As luck would have it, two feet of snow fell in Chicago the Tuesday before I was to fly out. My big brother, who has been a father figure to me since our father passed away, said, "Be careful. You know there are folks that don't want the truth to come out. Just tell what you know – set the record straight." My wife had parting words for me as well: "Be careful, you don't know these people. If this turns out to be some sort of media event, you don't know who's going to be paying attention." My wife had read more things about JFK's assassination over the years then I had, and we had all seen things on TV, but I could hardly believe that I would have all this contact with two men, who over a period of months, while trying to get a group of us together, would try to do us harm. I will say this: what I learned at the meeting in Westmont, Illinois, and my own private research since, has made me give more credence to my family's warnings.

The man who picked me up by prearrangement (Phil Singer had thought ahead about everything we would need during the visit, including the participant's being picked up and delivered to the hotel) escorted me into the lobby. He told me, "Phil and William are in the room," pointing the way. Stepping into the room, I had been directed to, was like stepping back into the 60s. There were two men sitting in hardback metal folding chairs casually talking to each other. One was bald, wearing glasses, clean shaven, and looking like an older version of a college football player – which I found out later, he had been. The other man was dressed casually in a long sleeved blue pullover sweater and jeans. His long gray hair was pulled back into a ponytail, and he sported a close cropped beard of the same color. They both noticed me at the same time and stood up to greet me. The fellow with the beard and ponytail turned out to be William Law, and, of course, I recognized Phil Singer as soon as he spoke. As soon as we had greeted one another, one of them said, "Let's get our cameraman in here to film right now."

They had me sit down in one of the many chairs that were in the room – the room had not yet been set up for filming and there was a certain amount of disarray in the furnishings. A man with a video camera seemed to appear out of nowhere. Phil and William started asking me questions and I told them how it all started for me. I told them about the helicopter ride, shadowing the motorcade – the ambulance taking off in the crush of reporters and picture takers jumping in the back of the pickup truck, having to go around the facility, finally finding the ambulance and taking the President's casket into the Bethesda morgue, and then guarding the morgue doors in shifts. Phil asked me at one point during the filming to go into another part of the room and asked me to stand at one of the doors to demonstrate how I was guarding the morgue door and how I was able to look in and see the president's body lying on the morgue table. Phil asked me to describe what

I saw when I looked into the morgue briefly. Phil Singer said "Hubie" and picked up a block, a plastic block, and handed it to me.

"Yeah," I said, "that's it."

Phil said, "This is a chock? That's it? This is what you saw? Something essentially like this?" I took the plastic block and demonstrated how it worked by putting it behind my own neck and holding it there.

Law said "Maybe not exactly like this, but," holding the block up I said "Yeah, but it's shaped like this." Again, I demonstrated by putting it behind my neck. "Not his head," I told them, moving the block to the back of my head, "but like this," moving the chock back behind my neck. "It raises the body up," and I tilted my head back. "It raises the upper chest so that when they do the "Y" incision, it's almost like that," I said, raising my chest up even more. I tilted my head and body way back in the chair I was sitting in to demonstrate what putting a block behind a deceased person's neck would do to the chest area.

I told them I had become familiar with what a chock block looked like when I was a police officer in New York and had to be in the morgue from time to time. I told them about seeing someone bringing in the President's burial suit, seeing the mahogany burial casket when the casket was delivered and the body was ready, wheeling the casket out of the morgue on a gurney, putting it in the ambulance, getting back into the pickup truck and following the ambulance back to the White House.

I was answering a question posed by William about the casket, after he read from the book, *The Death of a President*, describing how we had taken the casket out of the ambulance, when I saw Tim Cheek come through the door. He stuck his hand out and I said, "Hey," and got up and shook his hand. I thought, "I'm seeing my brother after 51 years." Tim introduced me to his wife DeeDee and we gave each other a hug. Tim looked just as I remembered him. His hair had thinned on top, and he had gone gray. He was older, as was I, but he still had the military bearing of the Marine he once was. We talked about the flight in, and how cold the weather was. William finally managed to get us to sit down together. Sitting across from Tim Cheek and me, William said to Tim:, "I apologize for doing this, because you just walked in and sat down, just having seen each other after 51 years."

I said, "That's okay."

Tim looked at William. "It's okay," he said smiling. "We've been up since three, so if I nod off… that's 3 o'clock our time in Florida."

William smiled and said, "That's perfect."

Tim and I sat back and waited for William's question. "I was just asking Hubie about the casket entry [into the Bethesda Naval Hospital]. Holding up the book, *The Death of a President*, by a man named William Manchester, Law said, "This supposedly gives the official version, and I wanted to read it to you and get your thoughts on it."

Before William could start reading, I broke in with, "When you say the official version, the…"

He said, "Let me tell you. *The Death of a President* written by William Manchester, The Kennedys hired him to write the official biography of everything that happened [that weekend]. There came to be problems down the road and they got into a big fight. Supposedly, when Manchester was writing this book, this was the writer's interpretation. He was allowed to talk to all the Kennedy's, people that knew the Kennedy's, so he was basically the first person to write what this…"

"So," I said, "when you say that he spoke to the Kennedy's whom did he research it with? Are there things that we know?" I motioned with my hand back and forth between Tim and me and shook my head.

"Well," Tim broke in with, "if you're going to quote something, we will figure it out."

William said, "Well, let me read this to you and get your impressions. I want to know basically, if this is your memory of the event." William Law began to read from Manchester's book, *The Death of a President*, page 399:

The muddle was the consequence of a failure in interservice communication. The Army had been as vigilant as the Navy; General Wehle stationed himself beyond the cornerstone in a staff car, with Lieutenant Bird and his body bearers right behind him in a truck. They had observed Mrs. Kennedy's arrival, but the darkness, the great blocks of silent people, and the many moving vehicles distracted them. It had confused two Naval physicians, too. When an ambulance drew away from the curb they called, "That's it—we'll guide you to the morgue." At the morgue Wehle, Bird and the six enlisted men debarked and inspected each other's uniforms while awaiting some movement from the ambulance. It was still as still. The Lieutenant crept up and peered inside. It was empty. Even the driver had gone. Panicky, they fled back and saw, among the shining cat's eyes, the uneasy face of Godfrey McHugh. Wehle and Bird colored. The military District of Washington was meticulous about ceremony; for a casket team to leave a Commander in Chief's casket was an astounding lapse, and after casting about bitterly – and vainly – for the two doctors, they re-formed the tiny escort

The morgue was fronted by a concrete jetty approached along the left side by a short flight of cement steps. Since coffins were the most precious burden to pass this way the stairs should've been designed for them. They weren't. They were too narrow, and a steel handrail was an impediment to bearers. The railing thwarted the gesture of McHugh's. This once, he thought, it would be appropriate for a general to join hands with five enlisted men, and relieved the Coast Guardsmen in the team. But navigating the ponderous Britannia required exceptional dexterity on the left. McHugh was too old. He tried, and kept trying until his eyes filled with frustration. It was no use. He was holding them all up, and motioning to the lanky Coast Guard youth he capitulated. The others moved quickly then, inside and sharp left through the double brown doors labeled "RESTRICTED – AUTHORIZED PERSONNEL ONLY." Lieutenant Bird decided that he wasn't an authorized person. After his men had lowered the casket to a wheeled gurney he shepherded them into the corridor and mounted guard. Two Navy corpsman pass, rolling a litter. Nothing appeared to be on it except the small lump wrapped in sheeting. "What's that?" he inquired. "Baby. Born dead," one mumbled. The Lieutenant whispered, "Oh." It occurred to him that Bethesda wasn't going to be at all like Arlington.

Tim and I listened carefully. Law finished reading. Tim said "Well, I remember going up [the steps] with the hand railing in the way. I remember us having to that we were at first – could not find the casket it wasn't where we thought it would be. As to all of that, I don't remember a general… the lanky coast guard youth, that would have been [Bud] Barnum." Tim and I had talked about this prior to coming to Chicago.

I said, "Do you remember when we were standing in front of the hospital waiting for the ambulance to pull up? We had taken a helicopter from Andrews Air Force Base, so we were waiting for the ambulance to pull up, and as the ambulance pulled up, reporters and flashbulbs came from everywhere and the ambulance took off!" I looked at Tim and chuckled. "And that's when Lieutenant Bird said, "Hop in the truck!" And we were chasing it around the grounds. We were in sight of the ambulance for the first couple of minutes and then we lost it. I was thinking to myself, "Why is this ambulance going so fast?" There wasn't a lot of light or anything. It was like they were trying to lose us. We went around the complex and when we saw the loading dock there was someone out there and Lieutenant Bird stuck his head out and said, "Did you see an ambulance go by?" and the guy on the dock said, "No." We went back to the hospital and the ambulance wasn't there, so we went back around again to the back of the hospital at the loading dock, and the ambulance was there at the loading dock. I don't know where it had driven off to previously or what route the ambulance driver had taken, but it should have been there during our first time following it to the back of the hospital, but it wasn't."

William asked Tim to tell of his memories of us losing the ambulance. "I remember it wasn't where it was supposed to be when we first got there. As to whether it was lost, I don't know." Tim used his fingers to make air quotes. "Either it wasn't where it was supposed to be or we weren't where we were supposed to be. We had gotten in a truck or something and we drove around looking for it." I looked at William, smiling and nodding in the affirmative.

William said to Tim, "Have you got an estimate on how long that would have been, that you were looking for it?"

Tim said, "I would say no longer than half an hour at the most." I didn't understand why William Law kept asking about us chasing the ambulance around the complex that night, but I would soon learn why, and that information would change my life.

Chapter Eight

RECOGNIZING DECEPTION

During the session with Singer and Law, after Tim and I shared our memories of those four tragic days, I decided to take my things to my room and take a break. When I came back James Felder, another of my honor guard brothers was there. As with Tim Cheek, seeing Felder took me right back to the night of November 22, 1963, when we first met climbing aboard the waiting helicopter at Andrews Air Force Base. Felder looked ... well, like Felder. He had aged gracefully, and like Tim, his hair was thinning on top, he was older but the only real difference was that his upper lip was now adorned with a mustache. We had time to reminisce for a bit before we all retired to our rooms to rest and await the other members that were supposed to join us. Many of them I already knew by their names: Dennis David, James Metzler and James Jenkins. One more that was supposed to join us was not an honor guard brother, but a man who had ridden with us on the helicopter ride to the hospital from Andrews Air Force Base, Richard A. Lipsey, who was the aide to General Wehle. I learned later that his participation was in question right up until the last moment, as was Jim Metzler's, but they were here, and that's all that really mattered to me.

I peered down the length of the tables that had been put together so all of us could sit together. I sat at the end of the table with Phil and William and my new friend Jim Jenkins. Dennis David was sitting further down the table with his wife Marion as was Tim and his wife DeeDee. James Felder sat amongst them, along with the camera crew that had been hired to film the next day's events. There were people to take still pictures as well. All in all, it was quite a crowd. Arrangements had been made to have dinner at one of Phil's favorite pizza joints. It was after all, Phil's home turf and he had gone to great lengths to make sure we were all comfortable. It was a good opportunity to renew old acquaintances and meet new ones. I really couldn't believe I was sitting at a table with people I hadn't seen in over five decades who were such an important part of my life and part of the history of this country. Meeting with the other men from the honor guard was my reason for leaving the sunshine of Atlanta, Georgia, for the 18 degree temperature of Chicago. As I sat there taking it all in, and as great a time as I was having, I couldn't help feel a tinge of sadness that Bud Barnum, Doug Mayfield, and Richard Gaudreau couldn't be there. Not to mention those who had passed on, Jerry Diamond and Larry Smith, and of course, Lieutenant Bird, to make it truly a reunion of the Kennedy Honor Guard.

During my brief first visits with Dennis David and his wife Marian, both I figured were in their late 70's, I found Dennis to be smiling and good-natured, as was his wife. They sat together at the dinner table, holding hands. Jim Metzler I found to be a quiet person with an easy smile that put me at ease immediately. James Jenkins was so quiet that I sometimes had to lean forward to hear him when he spoke. He had a genuine smile and had a very warm personality. Richard Lipsey, all these years later, too looked the same to me, just an older version of the man I held in memory. I found him in animated conversation with Tim and DeeDee and a fellow named Glen Bybee, one of the photographers. The festivities lasted late into the evening. It was decided at the end of dinner to take pictures of those of us that were at Bethesda Naval Hospital that night, 51 years before. A toast was given to the "Bethesda seven." It was decided by group consensus that we would not sleep in. We would get an early start in the morning and would all gather early the next morning to discuss what we each had experienced while on duty that night of November 22, 1963. Despite the excitement, it had been a long day and when we all returned to the hotel I went straight to my room, got undressed, turned back the bed covers, climbed in and slept like the dead.

The next morning, two tables had been put together into an inverted V. Tim sat at the end, to the left of Dennis David. David sat next to me, Jim Jenkins sat to my left, and Jim Metzler sat next to Jenkins, on the right. Next was Richard Lipsey, and sitting at the other end of the V was James Felder. Phil Singer and William Law sat towards the back of the room. There were tall lights set up to illuminate the table where we sat. Five or six cameras were set up in front of us, as the event was being documented. As it turned out, Lipsey spoke first as he had to leave our group early to catch a plane to where he lived in Baton Rouge, Louisiana. Lipsey showed a short presentation that he had on his laptop computer that he had brought with him. I felt a little strange sitting there while it played, but what could I do but go with the flow?

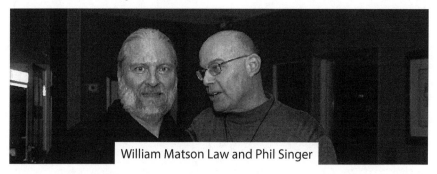

William Matson Law and Phil Singer

Lipsey talked about where he was when he heard the news that the President had been shot and what he did at the Kennedy funeral. My ears perked up when he started talking about the honor guard – and climbing aboard the helicopter. "We went to Fort McNair. Our Chief of Staff had already pulled together the team, our team, and slowly but surely over the next 30 to 40 minutes, teams from everywhere: the third infantry of the Marine Corps, the Air Force, Navy, all the heads of those ceremonial people came and that's where we sat at Fort McNair. All afternoon waiting word for what time they would ship the body back, and I think they were even planning to send an honor guard to Texas, but it never happened because they left Parkland as you know, and went straight back out on the airplane and started home and that's when we got the ETA [estimated time of arrival] around 6:30 or so, somewhere around there. That's when we headed out. By then, we had the facts of what we had to do. They had told us that the autopsy would be done at the hospital – Bethesda Naval Hospital. So, we had the parade route planned out and we got into that banana helicopter – I call it banana, the big helicopter – [Lipsey rotated his hands and twirled his fingers of his hands for emphasis] I didn't know it was going to have that many people in it – it ended up having the Third Infantry Honor Guard, the General [Wehle] and myself and the Marine Honor Guard. The Marines had 14 or 15 members of the Marine Honor Guard, and that thing was huge." This bit of information fit nicely with what I remembered and I was now glad that Richard Lipsey had gone first out of our group.

Lipsey continued, "[during my presentations] I talk a little bit about what I did at the autopsy, I don't talk about what I saw, because there is no reason to get into that kind of detail. To me, that's always been kind of confidential. I've talked about it more among friends and different things, and there has been some different quotes [from me]. Of course you can listen to what I said to the HSCA, you know, afterwards. I'm not sure all who had to sign it, but somebody from the State Department came into the autopsy room – I sat there during the autopsy and waited for Gawler's funeral home to come in, and then sat there the whole time Gawler's put him back together- and I signed a statement that I wouldn't say anything for 15 years of what I saw in that room and so I didn't. "

Lipsey continued, "Fifteen years and maybe one or two days later I went down to my office at eight in the morning to open up and there was a black sedan parked in front and two guys got out of the sedan and said, 'Are you Richard Lipsey?' I said 'Yes.' They said, 'We're from the HSCA and we want to interview you about the autopsy [of President Kennedy]'. Well, it's been 15 years, they told me not to talk to anybody about it, it totally caught me off guard, you have got to remember details [from] 15 years ago when you really purposely have put it out of your mind." (Lipsey had interlocked the fingers of both of his hands and was holding them up off the table in front of him for emphasis), because that wasn't very – I'm sure to all of you that had anything to do with it [Lipsey now folded his arms across his chest] that experience was a very personal experience – that's what I treasured, not the horrible incident that a president was shot, but to be part of those four days, having known him while I was in Washington, and I saw him so many times. So, anyhow, I wanted to record it [meeting with the men from the HSCA] you know, because… and they said 'Fine, but we're going to record it too.'"

Lipsey seemed amused telling us this, smiling and chuckling. "So they went out to the car, they got a tape recorder, recorded it, so"… [Lipsey looked out at the people in the darkened back part of the room where Law, Singer and Robert Groden and some others sat, and nodded his head towards them.] "I'm sure everybody here has listened to it. I didn't even remember … I listened to it years ago. I don't even remember what I said during that thing. I was in kind of a state of shock."

I sat there fascinated by Lipsey, sharing some of his memories of what had happened after we took the body of the President to the White House. I had been there for most of that, so it wasn't all that important to have Richard tell me about it. Despite Lipsey telling us he never discussed with people about what he had seen in the morgue, he did share a bit of what he experienced. "After the autopsy, I was still sitting in the room, but I'd gone out and gone to the bathroom and I came back in and General Wehle came down [Lipsey put his head back and looked up at the ceiling, raising his hands] and handed me a hamburger and a Coke." Richard looked at all of us with a "can you believe it?" expression on his face. Some of our group chuckled and with amusement in his voice. Lipsey said, "Here I am, sitting in an autopsy room, looking at the President of the United States on that table, and he hands me a hamburger. I'd never seen a dead man before, much less the president of the United States! I admit – it wasn't very appetizing, but at that point, I stepped out in the hall and ate the hamburger and went back in the morgue and then I watched Gawler's funeral home prepare the President's body." Richard then claimed that he helped Gawler's dress the President's body and help put him in the casket. I didn't know what to think when I heard Richard Lipsey tell us that, but he had been in the morgue and I had not, so who was I to say?

Law directed that James Felder tell his story next, and after him, Dennis David. I didn't really know who Dennis David was. I knew that Law had brought them into the "reunion" but all I knew besides that was that he had something to do with the morgue. David told us where he grew up, how he wanted to be in the military and how he came to be stationed at Bethesda Naval Hospital. It was interesting and I was learning, as was the rest of the group. Felder and Lipsey seemed to be paying very close attention to what Dennis was telling us, from what I remember from the looks on their faces. Tim, sitting to Dennis David's right, had an impassive look on his face.

Then I heard Dennis David say, "I had six or seven men off my duty station and had them report to me over at the main building. I assigned them different spots and gave them the information of what the Secret Service had stated. Then about 6:30, I got a call that said, 'Your visitor is on his way, we need help to offload.'"

I noticed at this point in Dennis David's narrative, Felder and Lipsey were listening intensely, as was Jim Metzler. Jenkins was sitting quietly as was Tim Cheek, and I didn't know what to think. Then came this: "I had been called over to the barracks again, I had three men left from my duty section, so then I called the chief of the day of the dental school, we happened to be pretty good friends," and I said, 'I need some help. Have you got any extra men?' He said, "How many do you need?" I said, 'Three would be great.' He said: 'Where do you want them?' I said, 'I want them on the jetty down at the morgue ASAP.' He said, 'They'll be there.'"

Dennis continued, "I then went down, which took maybe five or six minutes to get them from where I was at, and before I could get all the way down there, the six Navy people who I needed, were gathering [within] minutes, three or four minutes. After they arrived, a black hearse pulled in, and five or six men in suits got out of the ambulance or the hearse in the back."

Jim Jenkins broke in and said, "Can I ask a question?" He then asked Dennis, "What type of casket came out of that … ?"

David replied, "A gray shipping casket, just like the ones we shipped out of Vietnam!"

Jim Jenkins then asked, "Did you witness delivery of another casket prior to that?"

"No," Dennis David answered. Dennis then continued with his narrative, "So then the men in the suits picked up this casket out of the ambulance, and slid it up onto the jetty. The jetty was probably 40 inches...."

Phil Singer asked, "That's like a concrete platform?"

Dennis answered, "No, it was a wooden platform. It was a loading dock about 40 inches off the ground. And they slid this shipping casket up to it. I had my men line up, pick it up, walk through the outside door entrance to the morgue, and about – 10 feet down perhaps [there were] double doors, they opened up, they carried this gray casket in and set it down on the dock."

I sat there listening to Dennis David, my mind reeling, but I was trying to remain calm looking, despite the shock I was experiencing. "On the dock?" I heard myself exclaim to David.

"On the floor" David answered.

Phil Singer broke in with, "On the floor of the anteroom?" Phil asked.

"On the floor of the anteroom, yes." David replied.

"They brought it from the jetty, through the double doors into the anteroom? Which is outside the morgue?" Phil said.

"Yes," David reiterated, "which is outside the morgue. It's actually not in the morgue, it's adjacent to the morgue?" Phil questioned. "Yes," I heard Dennis David say.

Dennis went on to tell us that he sent his men off back to their barracks. He then described the men who had been driving the black hearse as being dressed in "scrubs." "They weren't military. Their clothes, the pants they had on were not uniform, and their shoes were neat. I just had the feeling they were not military [men]." David said that he talked to the driver of the hearse and he told Dennis David, 'We came up 10th Street, picked up Jones Bridge Road and came in the back way.'

David then told us that the entrance to Jones Bridge Road ran right by the officer's club. I was confused. A gray shipping casket? We the Honor Guard had delivered John F. Kennedy's body to the back of the loading dock to the Bethesda morgue at 8 P.M. We did not take the casket out of a black hearse – we had taken it out of a gray navy ambulance. I thought, "What in the hell is this guy talking about? Are you kidding me?" David started to say something else, but I interrupted with, "When you said that the men who were assigned to you, were they in blues or were they in hospital whites or…?

David answered: "They were in whites."

I said "Okay."

"They were all Navy, they were students just like Jim Metzler and I," Jim Jenkins broke in.

"We were all students" said Dennis David, trying to clarify it for me. I was still in a state of disbelief. All I could do was sit and listen and try to take it all in.

Phil Singer, who was leading the discussion for now said, "Because I think this will help; my understanding is that we are talking about three caskets, and let me describe them – just kind of hear me out. Dennis, there is a plain [metal] box shipping casket, which is not ceremonial, it's not what you would see at a funeral, it's just for transporting a body back from Vietnam like in the 60's." Dennis nodded in the affirmative. "Exactly," Phil Singer continued, "that's one type of casket and you saw that, and your six guys saw that?"

David replied, "Yes."

Phil said, "The second casket that we are talking about is the one that was in Dallas, it's called the bronze ceremonial casket, from the O'Neill funeral home – we see that loaded on Air Force One at Love Field in pictures – and we see it being unloaded at Andrews Air Force base into the gray navy ambulance and driven to Bethesda. That's the second casket, and that's the one with the damaged handle. Are we all in agreement?" We all nodded our heads. "The third is from Gawler's funeral home, and that's the big mahogany casket that weighed more than any casket ever carried in your life. It was clearly bigger and heavier than the bronze casket with the broken handle, and it was clearly not the shipping casket."

The get together in Chicago, Westmont to be exact – a suburb of Chicago – lasted one day. The session was long, lasting for many hours, late into the night. Most of us were scheduled to leave early the next day. Richard Lipsey left early in the session to catch his flight back to Louisiana. During a break Lipsey announced he had to leave. As he was leaving, despite all he had heard, he said, "I know there are some disagreements along the way about [the assassination] of Kennedy, but I will go on the record that he was shot from behind by Lee Harvey Oswald, twice in the head [Lipsey took his right hand and placed it on the right back part of his own head] and in the back and there is no hesitation in my mind or the doctors, who shot Kennedy. Now if there was a conspiracy – I don't think there was one – that's my personal opinion. I think he was a nut, and I can't… I've never found anyone who could trace it to anybody that guys, you know, that anybody else shot – that somebody else put Oswald up to it – but it could be, who knows? Kennedy was shot from behind by Lee Harvey Oswald, and there is every evidence in the world, to place it and not enough to displace it. Like Vince Bugliosi told me [Lipsey pronounced it Bellaougosie] there are 244 conspiracy theorist groups in the country, and every one of them think they are right. They all have a different opinion." With a shrug of his shoulders, Lipsey shook hands with William and Phil Singer, he said a few more words to the three of us left at the table, poured himself a glass of water and was gone.[1]

I was confused how Richard Lipsey could be the same man who uttered "there's something rotten in Denmark" to the HSCA members who came to see him and his company in Baton Rouge, Louisiana, who seemed to have doubts about events compared to the man we all met in Westmont Illinois. He so firmly believed Lee Oswald acted alone.

The Westmont meeting over, the next day, as I flew home to Atlanta, I pondered over what I had learned. There had been three casket entries that night at Bethesda Naval Hospital. The first event was about 18:35

---

1   I found Lipsey's behavior somewhat strange throughout the short time we spent with him, i.e. he helped straighten out one of President Kennedy's arms that was bent at the crook of the elbow, saying he helped dress the President, but it was increased when I got home and got a copy of Lipsey's 1978 HSCA testimony where he says, "there's something rotten in Denmark."

(6:35 P.M) military time based on the testimony of Dennis David, who gave orders to six or seven enlisted men. The enlisted men unloaded a metal shipping casket from a black Cadillac hearse which apparently contained the body of the late President. The men put the shipping casket on the floor of the morgue and left and went back to their posts. The second casket entry was at 7:17 P.M., this casket was unloaded from a marked gray Navy ambulance by Secret Service Agent William Greer and Roy Kellerman, and two FBI agents Francis O'Neill and James Sibert. They took the Dallas casket into the morgue. O'Neill and Sibert's testimony originally matched when they gave depositions to members of the House Select Committee in 1978. They were with Kellerman and Greer. O'Neill changed his testimony before the Records Review Board in 1997 and said he helped to take JFK's body in with the honor guard to conform with the official entry of the Dallas casket being brought in with the honor guard at 8 P.M. Sibert never changed his testimony from what he told the HSCA in 1978 or the Records Review Board in 1997. So how can the FBI version be believed if one of the agents is willing to change what he actually saw or did? Where is the truth? Can it be found? I think now, that the ambulance chase, for lack of a better word, had more than a little to do with how there were different casket entries at different times into the Bethesda morgue. I can't say I know how the conspirators managed it. We went around the grounds at least two, maybe three times. It was dark and cold and we couldn't see much from the back of the pickup truck we were in I don't know where the ambulance we were chasing went – the ambulance driver had to take a different route than we did – because we would have found the ambulance if we were just chasing each other around the grounds. But we didn't. The gray Navy ambulance was just backing up to the morgue loading dock at the back of the morgue at the second or third lap around the complex. Were we distracted chasing the ambulance for 15 to 20 minutes to give the powers that be time to have Kellerman and Greer and O'Neill and Sibert – without the FBI agent's knowledge – to bring in an empty casket from Dallas so that we could bring it in again at 8 P.M.? I don't know.

I remembered what Tim Cheek had told William Law: "I remember it wasn't where it was supposed to be when we first got there. As to whether it was lost, I don't know. Either it [the ambulance] wasn't where it was supposed to be or we weren't where we were supposed to be."

After talking with the rest of the Honor Guard members who had not been able to be with the rest of us in Chicago, I went through a bit of depression. If we were used in some kind of deception to cover up what had happened to President Kennedy and from what I had learned at the meeting in Westmont, it seems more than likely. I don't think Bud Barnum or Richard Gaudreau or Doug Mayfield believed there was a plot to kill Kennedy or that anything had really been going on during the so-called ambulance chase, or delivering the bronze display casket from Dallas to the Bethesda morgue at 8 o'clock – but those fellows hadn't had the experience, Tim Cheek, James Felder and I had of listening to Dennis David and his story of giving orders to six or seven enlisted men to deliver a cheap metal shipping casket into the Bethesda morgue at 6:35 P.M. Nor did they hear from James Jenkins or Jim Metzler. These people had been in the morgue. I have listened carefully to all they said and I can say that their stories had the ring of truth.

I had listened to Richard Lipsey's story as well. We had been together on the helicopter shadowing the presidential motorcade that night in November, but I really didn't have any connection to him at the conference. He had told the tale of seeing President Kennedy's body on the autopsy table. Lipsey had said that the President's left arm had been bent up at the elbow and he had been asked to hold JFK's arm while an attendant got up onto the work table to straighten out the arm. I didn't buy it. Why would they ask Lipsey who was just there to observe events to go up to the autopsy table and help the morgue attendant when there were already trained medical people who were dressed in the appropriate scrub clothing? And there is the matter that no one else that was at the Chicago meeting saw anything like that. As a trained investigator with the NYPD for more than two decades, I've learned that if you interview people at an event and only one person describes something that all the others who saw the same event did not see, there is a lack of credibility, so I didn't buy everything I heard during the event in Westmont.

Top: The trees in the left are on the grassy knoll. Looking at Elm Street from the triple overpass. Bottom: Facing Elm Street from the grassy knoll.
Photos by Hugh Clark, 2015.

Chapter Nine

FEELING BETRAYED

After the event in Westmont, I continued my research into Kennedy's assassination. I read about Lee Harvey Oswald, his troubled childhood, how he was born two months after his father Robert Oswald died, and how his older brother Robert got away from home just as fast as he could, leaving Lee alone with their overbearing mother until, at the age of 17, he enlisted in the Marines. Oswald supposedly had dyslexia but wound up at Atsugi Air Force Base as a radar operator. There are many things I learned in research that surprised me. Oswald got a hardship discharge from the service, to help his ailing mother but then went to Russia. He was allowed to stay in Russia, got a job at a radio factory making more than the foreman of the facility, was allowed to marry a Russian woman whose uncle was a colonel in the Soviet military of internal affairs; The MVD (Ministry of Internal Affairs) was part of the Russian security police. After two years, Oswald was allowed back into the United States bringing his Russian wife with him and was questioned by no official except someone from the Travelers Aid Society, all at the height of the Cold War. Oswald landed in New Orleans with his Russian wife and child and, while he lived there, took a shot at General Edwin Walker, a right wing advocate. Oswald fired at Walker from a mere 20 feet away, but with the same rifle he shot at President Kennedy from over 200 feet and hit him? Never mind that Oswald hit the President more than once in six seconds. Nor do any of these aspects make sense: his supposed trip to Mexico City, or how Oswald just happened to get the job at the Texas school Book Depository, or how Oswald was shot after his capture at the Texas Theater, while in the custody of the Dallas police.

I'm not an intellectual, but I am someone with a good amount of common sense and detective experience. In the end it wasn't any of those things that made me believe Lee Harvey Oswald did not act alone, if in fact if he acted at all. It was the Zapruder film. I had seen it before, of course, but after the Chicago adventure I was sent a copy of the 26 second home movie of the Kennedy assassination taken that day by Abraham Zapruder. I paid close attention to every frame, seeing it through fresh eyes and a different mindset. At the moment of the head shot, President Kennedy is shot in the front right side of his head. Even if Oswald shot Kennedy from behind, explain to me how the back of his head is blown out. I'm not a hunter, but I have been at the crime scene of many gunshot/ suicides. I know and any hunter will tell you, that a bullet goes into a body, leaving a small wound of entry, and comes out leaving a big hole. When the President was hit in the head, he fell over on his left side and into his wife's lap. If the shot hit Kennedy from behind, it would have blown out part of his face. The photographs I was shown in Westmont, Illinois, showed no such damage. I'm no genius – but I am an ex-investigator with common sense and a good deal of training.

My life since having been a participant at the meeting in the Windy City has been filled with a burning desire to know what happened to our President. To try and learn what part I had unwittingly played in the aftermath in the deception of JFK's death to know how my honor guard comrades and I had been used. I still spent a fair amount of time on the golf course, but now my favorite pastime had to take a backseat to my obsession with the Kennedy assassination. Every time I read a new book on the assassination or see a new documentary about it, my indignation grows. Sometimes my wife would join me in watching something about the assassination and more than once I saw her with tears in her eyes.

My time in the military took me all over the world. The one place I had never been was the site of John Kennedy's murder, Dealey Plaza in Dallas, Texas. Now, at the age of 71, I thought I would never have the chance. I needed to see the area for myself. An investigator must always see the scene of the crime firsthand. I am a man of faith. My father after all, was a pastor. My prayer to go to Dealey Plaza was answered in the form of publisher Kris Millegan of TrineDay publishing.

As it turned out, William Law, one of the co-hosts of the Chicago gathering had a new edition of a book he had written to be published by Trine-Day publications and he called me and asked if I would read the book and consider writing the forward. "It's never been done before," William Law told me during a call. "Having a member of the Kennedy Honor Guard do the forward to the book might get people's attention." I read the book with the new material (Law had given me a copy of the old edition soon after I had arrived home to Atlanta) and I was pleased to see that included in the new addition was a piece written by Phil Singer, a kind of "teaser" for the documentary Phil and William were planning to produce of the film they had shot of the Westmont events. So I wrote the forward to the new addition to Law's book with great enthusiasm.

Soon after the book's publication, I was asked to go to Dallas to give a guest presentation with William and a man now considered a friend, James Jenkins. That's how I found myself in a room listening to a panel on the assassination say that the casket we had carried into the Bethesda Naval Hospital morgue had been loaded down with oxygen tanks.

It was a good conference. The people were warm and friendly, and seemed to want to know what I had to say. I, in turn, watched and listened and learned what researchers had to say on the subject of JFK's assassination.

Now, sitting there, listening to a panel discussion about how the casket team took a casket to the morgue and then it was filled with oxygen tanks, I couldn't stay quiet. I found myself getting up from my chair and walking towards the panel. The room was filled with people. I walked up to Kris Millegan, "Kris," I said. "You have to let me speak to this."

Kris cut in with "We're about to cut it off, Hubie."

"No, Kris," I replied, "you've got to let me speak. Look at all the people in the room. What the speaker is saying isn't right. I don't want all these people to walk out of here with the wrong information."

Kris Millegan looked at me for a long few seconds and said, "All right. Address it." Kris walked up to a standing microphone and said, "We actually have one of the persons here that carried that casket, Hubert Clark." The audience clapped and I heard one of the panel members say, "All right."

When I was in the military I was assigned to the United States Navy Honor Guard, and part of my job was the responsibility of training and carrying out military funerals. My last funeral in Washington DC was John F. Kennedy. Now I have documentation, I have pictures of the casket, along with six or five other military men. We could determine how much a casket weighed, because we buried over 250 people at Arlington. Now when I hear you say that the casket weighed 2500 pounds – that's not accurate. There were only six of us at Andrews Air Force base that took the bronze casket off the elevator truck and put it in a Navy ambulance. At no time, if there were oxygen bottles, they would have been clanging together. At one point during our evacuation of the remains from the elevator truck, we almost dropped the casket. Now there were only six of us at the time.

When we put the bronze casket into the ambulance, we shadowed it all the way to Bethesda Naval Hospital. At no time did that motorcade stop, because we were going at a high rate of speed, we were in a helicopter and we shadowed it. Now there at a point in time at Bethesda we left the ambulance for approximately 15 minutes. And again, the six of us were able to carry that casket. And at no time was there any clanging, and believe me there would have been clanging.

After the autopsy was done, the President was transferred to a mahogany casket which was 1300 pounds and the six of us couldn't carry it. And the president was in that casket, alright, because we placed him in the casket in the morgue. Six of us could not handle 1300 pounds, so you can see why I question the bronze casket weighing 2500 pounds, we could not have carried it.

As you can see that entire book is a copy of every aspect of President John F. Kennedy's funeral, so believe me when I tell you, believe me when I tell you, that at no time was the Bronze casket out of our sight. At no time, excuse me if I get a little emotional, I told you about betrayal. The entire time we were at Bethesda Naval Hospital, the only casket that was brought into the morgue while we were present, was the bronze casket. At no time did we handle a silver shipping casket. The only other casket that went into the morgue that night was a mahogany casket that weighed approximately 1300 pounds. The only casket that came out of the morgue that night was a mahogany casket that weighed 1300 pounds.

I have been asked by this gentleman Phil Singer, I don't want to take up your gentleman's time, but the difference between being an eye witness to something and hearing what somebody told you happened.

After 51 ½ years, this gentleman right here, Phil Singer, brought the casket team and the gentlemen that worked in the morgue together. And as I told you, we had no idea who was on the inside of the morgue and who was on the outside of the morgue. But when we came together, which the government didn't expect, because when we left Washington , I went overseas to embassy duty, the other guys went to Asia, somebody else went to Africa, so we never had an opportunity to sit down together as a group and talk about the experience. But when we came together, in February of this year, he'd never told us that we were going to tell a story, he just said, "I wanted to have a reunion with you guys." Now nobody had spoken to each other in 51 years, but now we told our story, about Andrews Air Force Base, Bethesda Naval Hospital, what we were so proud to do.

And then it was time for the corpsmen in the morgue to tell their story, and they started out by saying, "We don't mean to dispute what you're saying, but a half an hour before you got here, we took a silver shipping casket out of a black hearse, and we brought it into the morgue, and we set it on the floor, and we moved the President's body that was wrapped in sheets and we placed it on the table." Now you can imagine, the almost fight that we had, in terms of who was lying to whom, but they politely said, "We're not disputing what you did, we are merely telling you what we did." Now these are corpsmen, these are enlisted men – they have no reason to lie. But it was at that time, where we all began to look at each other and say, "What was the purpose, the man was dead." And you heard Jim Jenkins talk about not finding any fragmentation, not finding any trace evidence, well that's what a cop like me would look for. So it simply meant to us, that the body had already been sanitized. That it made a stop before it got to Bethesda Naval Hospital.

And what you didn't know, what you didn't know, that we found out, that I found out, at the time the autopsy was taking place, we had an opportunity to look in, to go in, and view this, and I refused to go in, but I did take a peek. And one of the things that I could see from the waist up was that there was a chock block under the President's neck. And I never forgot it, because for me it looked like the president was sleeping. Well when I got out of the military in 1966, I became a New York City detective, and one time to the visit to the morgue, I walked in and I started smiling, and my partner said, "What are you smiling for in the morgue?" And I said, "That's what I saw under the President's neck." And it wasn't until I came to Chicago, and quote unquote saw the official pictures of the president's autopsy, I said, "That's not what I saw," and if you remember what Jim Jenkins said, because he was in the morgue that night. He said, "We don't' even have that (chock block) at Bethesda Naval Hospital." Thank you.

I finished speaking, thanked the people, put the microphone down and walked back to my seat. My anger had subsided, but the fire in my heart still burned. Still does.

I don't know what I was expecting after I walked the two blocks from my hotel to the Plaza. In the Zapruder film of the assassination, the Plaza looked enormous, at least a couple of football fields long and wide. But seeing it from where I was standing – at the corner of the plaza where the President's limousine pops into view in the Zapruder film, straight ahead was a shockingly small area. I continued to walk in the Plaza. I noticed there was a slight decline of the road something I couldn't tell from the Zapruder film. I stopped for a moment unsure what to look at first. I walked up the incline of the grassy Knoll; there was a long plaque and I read what was inscribed there:

> We in this country, in this generation, are – by destiny rather than choice – the watchman on the walls of world freedom. We ask, therefore, that we may be worthy of our power and responsibility – that we may exercise our strength with wisdom and restraint – and that we may achieve in our time and for all time the ancient vision of 'peace on earth, good will toward men.' That must always be our goal – and the righteousness of our cause must always underlie our strength. For as was written long ago…"except the Lord keep the city, the watchman waketh but in vain.

I knew enough by doing research at this time, to know the quote on the plaque was from JFK's undelivered speech that he was to give at the Trademart on November 22, 1963.

I walked over to the spot where Abraham Zapruder had stood on the small four foot pedestal when he took the now famous film. I took my hand and swept it over the surface. It looked like it had a fresh coat of paint applied in the not too distant past. I walked a few feet up the Knoll to my right and found myself inside the cement structure that I later learned was called the pergola. I walked down its length from the inside and I encountered Robert Groden whom I had met in Chicago. We greeted each other. I then stepped off the cement and onto the grass and walked behind the picket fence. I stood at the corner and then walked down seven or eight feet to where a gunman may have stood and fired the shot that had hit President Kennedy in the right side of his head. I stood there taking it all in. I turned my head left and looked at school book depository. I shifted my eyes to the spot in the street where Kennedy had been shot, the last fatal shot that blasted out the back of his head. I had, by now, read James Humes cryptic statement before the Warren commission. Allen Dulles had asked Humes if Kennedy's head wound was consistent from a shot from behind JFK. Humes had replied, "Scientifically sir, it is impossible for it to have been fired from other than behind, or to have exited other than from behind."

As I stood there behind the picket fence looking at the street, I knew it was all bullshit. A shot from where I was standing was perfect for what was on the Zapruder film. JFK was hit in the head, and his head went back to the left and Kennedy fell into his wife's lap. I shook my head in disbelief. I thought, "No wonder people have been so stirred up about this for fifty years. No one could stand here behind this fence and think anything else but that he was shot from here."

I turned around and looked behind me at the parking lot. I remembered the story of Lee Bowers, who said he had been in the tower before the assassination. I had recently seen Mark Lane's 1966 film, *Rush to Judgment*, and I heard Lee Bowers' voice in my head as I looked at the tower, "At the time of the shooting… There was a flash of light or it was something which occurred which caught my eye on the immediate area on the embankment. Now what this was I could not say at that time and at this time I could not identify it other than there was some unusual occurrence, a flash of light or smoke which caused me to feel like something had occurred there." Bowers was then asked by Lane to give the spacing of the shots he heard which in Bowers opinion were three. "There were three shots and they were spaced with one shot, a pause and then two shots in very close order, such as," perhaps Bowers took his right hand and knocked on the table he and Lane were sitting at: "knock – knock knock, "almost on top of each other while there was some pause between the first and second shots…. When I stated I felt like the second and third shots could not have been fired from the same rifle, the [FBI] reminded me I was not an expert." I had to agree. "Yeah, I'll bet," I said aloud. I turned back around for one more look at the view of the street. I walked back from behind the picket fence and found myself at the top of some cement steps that led down from the Knoll to the street. It had a handrail all the way from the top of the steps to the bottom. I didn't recognize it from watching the Zapruder film, so I could only surmise it was fairly new. The metal rail was hot to the touch as I put my hand out to steady myself as I walked carefully down the steps. As I made the slow walk down the steps, I couldn't help thinking of that other slow walk, step by step, so very long ago up the steps of the capital and down slowly step-by-step and then the long walk where the world watched as we took John Fitzgerald Kennedy to his final resting place.

On the sidewalk, I was surprised to see a small metal plaque embedded at the edge of the grass at the curb. It described Dealey Plaza as an historical landmark. The date on the plaque was 1993. I looked up from the plaque to see a large white X in the street. I realized the X marked where John Kennedy had been hit by that last fatal shot to his head. I stood there mesmerized, looking at the X in the street. Traffic was almost nonexistent. I stepped off the curb and walked a few steps and stood directly on the white marker. I was facing the triple overpass. I now knew there had been several people on the overpass during the assassination, including men who work at the railroad, Elmer Todd and his supervisor S.M. Holland. These men both saw smoke floating above the trees from the picket fence where they were standing on the overpass. I'm glad they were there because we wouldn't have their testimonies now and thank God for Mark Lane and his film *Rush to Judgment*, because I wouldn't have been able to sit in my living room and watch Holland or Todd give their testimony to Lane. I'm an eye to eye guy. Every investigator on a case needs to be able to see the person's face and observe his expressions as he tells his story. You have to be able to see how he holds his body. I wasn't able to do all of this, of course, but Lane's film took me closer than I would have been able to get otherwise. Now that having been said, no one should have been able to be on the overpass except law enforcement. It had been sloppy, sloppy police and Secret Service work.

I turned around, still standing directly on the X in the street. I now faced in the direction of the book depository. I raised my right arm checking the trajectory and angle from where I was standing. I turned and now faced the grassy knoll and did the same. For 50 years I believed Lee Harvey Oswald shot Kennedy. But now, standing right on the spot where he had been shot, I couldn't buy it. The first lesson a policeman learns is to protect the crime scene. Double the perimeter of the scene to make sure everything is protected, everything. Speak to every witness separately, so their stories are untainted with another witness's visual and verbal memories. The crime scene in Dealey Plaza was not protected. Why were people who were not certified law-enforcement allowed on the overpass? Why were people allowed to trample the area behind the picket fence tainting any evidence that may have been found? Why were no law-enforcement officials standing behind the fence on the Knoll in the first place to make sure no one could take a shot at President Kennedy from that spot? It was a perfect place to shoot from. How could JFK have been allowed to be brought in to an area like this? I felt anger boiling inside. It was all here; the witnesses, the puff of smoke or flash of light at the time of the assassination; men on the overpass who had seen smoke on the Knoll behind the fence; the head snapped back and to the left.

Oswald supposedly took a shot at right wing General Edwin Walker at his home. Oswald who was hiding, watched Walker read a newspaper 20 feet away and fired at him and missed. Now here standing at the very spot where Kennedy was shot, facing the school book depository, I was to believe that Oswald fired from the 6th floor window, 250 feet away, at a moving target and hit him. "No way in hell," I said to myself.

I had spent my time since coming back from Westmont, Illinois, in February 2015, immersing myself in books on the assassination, looking at documents on the assassination. I had even gone back to Chicago under the auspices of Phil Singer in September of the same year, where I met Abraham Bolden who was the first black Secret Service agent hand-picked by the President himself. I met him at his home and found him to be a nice sincere man who told me of his time in the agency where he was treated terribly by his fellow agents. Racism was rampant at that time in the Secret Service. Not all were guilty of racism, I'm sure, but enough. I also met with Antoinette Giancana, daughter of the Chicago mob boss, Sam "Momo" Giancana. When I met Antoinette, she asked me right off the bat, who I thought killed her father. I was by now, familiar with the story of Sam Giancana, who was killed in the basement of his own home while cooking sausage and peppers. He was to testify before the HSCA in the next few days. But someone made sure he would never testify by putting a .22 bullet behind his ear and several around his mouth, an old Sicilian warning to keep your mouth shut. I looked at her and said, "I think he was killed by the CIA." Antoinette, who was about 80 years old at the time, looked at me with a twinkle in her eye and said, "Fucking right!"

The mechanism put in place to protect the most important man in the world broke down. How does something like this happen? The Dallas police force was supposedly the best in the country. Watching the Orville Nix film, I noticed that the motorcade officers – who were riding at the side of the President's limousine, towards the back, after the President had been shot, dropped back to where they were not even really near the car. What was that all about?

As I have previously stated, the most important thing I learned as an investigator is to protect the perimeter, in essence to protect the evidence. This was not done in the most important murder case in history. The building where Oswald supposedly shot Kennedy was not entirely closed off. Cartridges that were found near the 6th floor window, Captain Fritz picked up before they could be tested for fingerprints – it was said for years that Captain Fritz took no notes of the Oswald interrogation, only to have a bunch of notes suddenly be found and given to the Records Review Board. I recalled reading that when Fritz was questioned by the Warren commission, he said he took no notes at the time of all the Oswald interrogation, but made some notes days later. Protection of the crime scene, the evidence i.e. chain of custody of the evidence, was not protected. I don't care if it was a bunch of "good old boys" from Dallas,Texas, procedure is procedure, and they should have known exactly what to do. And they blew it, as did the agents of the Secret Service. Senator Ralph Yarborough in his Warren Commission affidavit said, "After the shooting … all of the Secret Service men seemed to me to respond very slowly, with no more than a puzzled look … I am amazed at the lack of instantaneous response from the Secret Service." I was angered to learn the Secret Service destroyed their trip reports, for September through November 1963, when the Records Review Board asked for them.

I stood on the big white X in the street, feeling the warmth of the Texas sunshine, something President John Kennedy never got another chance to do. My emotions were like a roller coaster inside of me. I looked at the grassy knoll and then back to the school book depository. How did they let this happen? Why did this happen? There was only one answer: betrayal, the betrayal of the President. The betrayal of every God-fearing man, woman and child in 1963, who believed in a thing called democracy. The betrayal continues to this day. By the acquiescence of the media and the propagandist who continue to spew out the pablum of "one man from a building, killed another man in a car." John F. Kennedy was not perfect. Neither is our system of government, but our system, our government, allowed John Kennedy to be the man he became. He was a leader for his time. A man, who was not virtuous, but could lead others toward virtue. This country allowed me, a black kid from the streets of New York to grow up to live a good life, to have certain values and ideals, and when fate found me at a place in history when I was called to do my duty, I did my very best, along with my comrades, to take my commander-in-chief to his place of rest. I'm going to continue to search for the truth of the assassination. I owe John Kennedy that. And so does his country.

APPENDIX A

Funeral Protocols

Law: So tell me the high ranks that got that. What rank did you have to be to get that sort of funeral?

Clark: Admiral and above.

Law: Admiral and above, so- so name- name me the – I'm not all that familiar with- with military – I mean, you'd have to be an Admiral, a General, something like that.

Clark: Oh, okay, so Admiral would be the equivalent to a General, all right?

Law: Okay.

Clark: But- but with- with- in the Navy, where you would see, like, two bars or one bar, that would be a Lieutenant, an army Marine Corps in the Navy one gold bar would be an Ensign and in the other military- in the other military he would be like a first Lieutenant. And then once you got a- a silver bar you would be a Lieutenant JG, and then the other military it would be a Lieutenant; you'd be like a full Lieutenant. And then with two bars, in the Navy, it would be a Lieutenant, but in the Army in the Marine Corps he would be a Captain, all right?

Law: Okay.

Clark: And with two and half bars in the Navy he would be a Lieutenant-Commander, where in the other military – other services, he would be like a Major.

Law: Okay.

Clark: All right?

Law: Now-

Clark: So the thicker the bar, in the Navy, like in our unit we – he was a Commander.

Law: Okay.

Clark: Okay? So, his name was Commander- Lieutenant-Commander McNulty, and he- he was hot so very low-key guy, very polished, and I believe he was from the northeast, like, you know, not Boston but Maine, you know, New Hampshire, Vermont, in that area. But he was a cool guy.

Law: This was the guy that was leading the funerals at that time?

Clark: Right, right, and he- he would be, on a Admirals funeral, he would be the Commander in charge, but anything lower than that, Lieutenant Simon Knight is- would lead it.

Law: Okay.

Clark: So the higher the rank, the higher the person in charge.

Law: I got you. So during this period of time you were just watching all of this, correct?

Clark: Well, yeah. I- I was watching but depending on how big the funeral was I would be one of the members of the entourage, you know, the guard carrying- I would be part of the members carrying the rifle.

Law: So you weren't-?

Clark: At the navy funeral, all the guards other than the pallbearers would be carrying, you know, would- would have their rifles and leggings on, you know, as part of- part of the contingent.

Law: Got you, so you weren't carrying coffins during this period of training, you were carrying your rifle and-?

Clark: My first- my first month, no.

Law: Okay.

Clark: So, but then after my first month, I mean, I- I really- I really learned, you know, all the funerals, all the, you know depending upon what- what funeral it was there were times what we call 'the chapel service' if they had, like, a chapel service. Other than leaving the remains that the gravesite, what we would call 'the chapel service' where we would leave the remains there in the chapel inside all at the cemetery. And the chapel service, we would have to meet the hearse at the chapel, take it out of the hearse, bring it into the chapel, after the service we would go down and we would retrieve the remains, bring it back out, put him in- back into the hearse, and then follow it to the gravesite where we did there before, like, a block before we reached the gravesite, the pallbearers would speed ahead, jump out, and be there to greet the hearse when it arrived. And then all the other cars, by the time all the people would- would- would arrive, we would wait for the family to be seated at the gravesite –

Law: Okay.

Clark: By the- by the time the family would- would get out of the cars the team would already have the remains on the gravesite with the flag above the casket. Once the family gets settled, then the services start where the pastor or the Chaplin would do the funeral and then he would look at me or look at the usher – whoever was in charge of the detail – he would look at the usher, the usher would look at the casket-team and nod his head, and then we would start polling the flag.

Law: Okay, so- so just for my own edification – I might use this – take me from the lowest kind of funeral- I want- I want to know that from the lowest ranking person, describe their funeral to me, and then maybe a middle person, and then the highest ranking. Explain that. Explain the procedures to me.

Clark: Okay, so for enlisted man, what he would get- I mean if he wanted a chapel service, he would get a chapel service.

Law: Okay.

Clark: All right? Same- same procedure, but he wouldn't have a contingent of, you know, guys with rifles, you know, walking to the gravesite – he wouldn't have that. He would just have the firing party and the casket-team, okay?

Law: Okay.

Clark: That would be for a regular enlisted man.

Law: Okay.

Clark: All right, now, for a Chief- for a Chief's funeral, that would be like an E7, all right? That would be a Chief. He would have- the Chief would be in charge of the details, okay? A Chief would be in charge, somebody of the equivalent rank as the person being buried-

Law: Okay.

Clark: – and he would have a contingent of- of guys, you know, maybe- maybe a- a small, like, I'd say, like maybe 20 guys for a Chief's funeral, okay?

Law: Okay.

Clark: And he'd have pallbearers and a firing party, all right?

Law: And that's how he would go to the grave, okay?

Clark: Now, for- for an Officer, an Officer would have a platoon of men, pallbearers, a firing squad, and an Officer would be in charge of- of the detail.

Law: Okay.

Clark: Now, for a Line Officer, meaning Admiral and above, you know, you could have a Rear Admiral, Vice Admiral, and if you had a full Admiral, they would have what we call Eighty seven; a full complement of the honor guard.

Law: Give me the full compliment. What would that consist of?

Clark: That would consist of 87 guys all in full dress blues. Eighty Seven, then you would have eight pall bearers, one usher, firing party and a commander leading the detail.

Law: Okay is that it?

Clark: That's it.

Law: That is how the funerals with rank went.

Clark: Right. With rank. Everybody had a pall bearer and the firing squad.

Law: Can you explain to me the significance of the firing squad. Why do they fire off their rifles?

Clark: It is an acknowledgment of a fallen warrior and it's like his final salute. After we would get the remains at the graveside, the flag would be over the casket, the funeral would go on and there are certain things that we would do just to reach the end because the flag had to be   a b o v e the remains so you wouldn't want to have it sagging or touching the casket, because once you take it off, it would be a sign of disrespect to have it sloping down on the casket. So what would happen is we would give each other different signals when we wanted to switch. We would, tag on the flag, so we knew that okay, it's time to change hands. Sometimes your hand would start to cramp up from holding it so tight, so we would hit the hands, and then we would be able to relax a little bit – one side would relax while the other side held it.

Law: I see, that is very interesting to know.

Clark: After the chaplain or the pastor would finish the funeral, the funeral director would look at the usher and nod his head and the usher would walk over to the family and say "At this time, the firing party Will fire three volleys which Will be followed by taps." The usher would then turn and salute the firing party, or the person that is in charge of the firing party, meanwhile, all the time its going on the firing party would be standing at parade rest. And then the person in charge of the firing party would say "Fire party, Attention." They would turn to attention. Then he would say "Fire Party, come to the range" and then the firing party would, I mean – they had this procedure, they would swing to the middle, up their rifles, and then the person in charge would say, "Aim, Fire, Aim, Fire, Aim Fire" and then he would say "present" and then the firing party would then spin back to the middle, and then he would say "Arms," and then they would present arms. And then we would start folding the flag. And then the taps would be blown.

Law: Explain the folding procedure to me.

Clark: What would happen is we would step forward and those on the head would turn, the left side, would fold the flag. Everybody has their hands on the flag. Nobody lets go. We would step forward and the guys on the right would take almost like a fold, we would fold it and then we would fold it again, then the guys at the foot would take the measurement about a foot and a half and then they would turn the flag up where we start the fold. Each individual, each pall bearer would take a fold and once he takes his hold he slaps down back down to its entry. It goes all the way up to the head, that means the stars, where the stars are. They then take the measurements once the fold comes all the way up, He takes the fold, he measures, he turns the upper portion in, and then we fold it where there is no red showing and when there would be no red showing the pall bearer would tuck it in. He then turns to the funeral director, and really snaps it out to the funeral director. Once the funeral director takes it, he holds it in front of the pall bearer, the pall bearer salutes it and turns back into the casket. The funeral director walks over to the family and presents it to the spouse.

Law: And that was how funerals were conducted there at Arlington.

Clark: Every day, the same procedure. It didn't matter whether you were an Admiral or a General or Private. Everybody received the same respect at the graveside.

Law: So now that you are done with your training, and you began your service there at Arlington.

Clark: My first funeral I was shaking in my boots. I was nervous but I knew what to do but it was the first time that I had ever handled a casket along with the team.

Law: So take me – whatever you can remember the first time you were doing that, give it to me step by step. If you have facts in your head you can remember or how you were feeling, tell me about that.

Clark: I remember we were sitting on a bus and I think it was Section 18 or Section 21 and we were sitting on the bus waiting for the hearse to show up. And as soon as we spot the hearse, we jump out, we form up, the firing party goes twenty yards away from the graveside and when it forms up, I was sitting on the bus and I was saying to myself, "I know I'd do this, I know I'd do this," and it wasn't like I was at the head and the foot, I was more or less in the middle, where most of the new guys started out because the head and foot were more responsibility. But because you are new, they put you in the middle, so whatever mistakes you made it could be covered up. But I just felt that I was ready. And I remember I was the only one looking out of the window and everybody else would be like not when they get, they said when we do see and I am looking out the window because I was nervous and I was the first one to spot it "there it comes." I was the first one off the bus and everybody else was taking their time because they knew their prize but I was excited because it was my first funeral. I was so cognoscente that the entire time the remains were pulling up, I was going through my head – okay you do this, you follow, if they say three paces, you take the three paces with no turning, and if they say four paces forward, then you take the four paces forward and then you turn in. But three paces simply means that you walk up three paces and stop. Three paces forward means you take three paces forward and turn in.

Law: What does turn in mean?

Clark: I was just trying to make sure that I had it right –

Law: When you –

Clark: – because sometimes –

Law: When you say turn in, what does that mean?

Clark: You turn in because once the hearse passes you, depending upon if it's on the right or the left, you turn either to the right or the left towards the back of the hearse.

Law: Okay. See, I have to explain this so people can see it visually in their head.

Clark: Right. So what happens is if the hearse pulls up, you're not right on top of it, you're about maybe four or five feet up from the hearse. You don't want the hearse to go by and it hits you so you're like back away. When the hearse pulls up and then the person in charge of the group Will say, "Body bearers, three paces forward." So we take three paces forward and then we go to Parade REST. What that means we had our back and then if we're not up to the hearse he'll say, "Body bearers, two paces forward." Then we go up two paces and then we automatically turn in towards the door of the hearse. Now we're facing the back of the hearse and then he'd say, "Body bearers, two paces." And two paces would bring us right up to the door of the hearse and the person in charge would open the hearse – open the door and then we would start to pull the remains out. And everything is done at attention. You don't – nobody's leaning over, everything is done at attention because you want to maintain military precision. That's the whole purpose of a military funeral, to let this be like the last respect for this guy. Nothing is done haphazardly. So when it comes out, we make sure that the flag is on right, we make sure that the foot always goes toward the gravesite first. The foot of the casket. The head is always where the blue is, that's the head of the casket. So when you're marching toward the graveside, you're taking like side-steps to get away from the hearse and then the person in charge of the funeral or of the pall bearers, he Will nod his head and then we'll start walking towards the gravesite. Once we get to the gravesite – the family is following – once we get to the gravesite, everybody's standing up and this is why – I don't know whether I said it but when you're – back at our barracks, we always had a weight rule because those caskets can be heavy and we would always in – how do you say it? We were always – when you want somebody to do something, you – Oh, we were always encouraged to lift weights. We'd do curls and stuff like that and lift weights because you never knew when you were going to get it heavy. And you had to be in shape because a lot of the times, when you got to the gravesite, you couldn't just drop the casket down, you had to slowly lower the casket. And if you had it heavy and you're doing it slow, you can hurt your back if you're not in shape.

Law: Right. You said you take the body with the heel towards the gravesite?

Clark: Right.

Law: Is that what – ?

Clark: We call head and feet. The feet always heads towards the casket. I mean towards the grave site.

Law: Okay, so how do you get it turned around to where the head is now where it needs to be? Do you – ? I'm not clear on the –

Clark: When we take it out of the hearse, we turn it. We take half steps and we turn to make sure that the feet is going toward the gravesite.

Law: Okay and so once you get to the gravesite, is that how it is? You just –

Clark: We side-step – once we get on the grave site, we side-step along because they have these boards on the gravesite and you just half-step – side-step onto the gravesite. Once we're all on the board then we slowly lower the casket onto the gravesite, onto that platform at the gravesite. Nobody comes up until we all have our hands on the flag and then we all come up together with the flag torn. And that's the way we stay until we get the nod from the funeral director.

Law: Okay. So if the feet –

Clark: After Taps, after the firing party then we fold the flag, hand it to the funeral director who then hands it to the family.

Law: I'm just trying to picture this in my head for my own edification. You're carrying –

Clark: It's beautiful.

Law: You're carrying the casket to the gravesite with the feet going first, right?

Clark: Right.

Law: So then you put it on the board and is the casket lowered that way?

Clark: No, no, no. They never lower the casket until the family leaves the gravesite.

Law: So when the family leaves the gravesite, is –

Clark: They pull the boards out from underneath the casket and it slips down into the grave but you never lower the casket while the family is at the gravesite. Sometimes it gets emotional. Sometimes, I've seen families throw themselves on the casket.

Law: I'm trying to get this straight in my head. So when we're at Arlington and we're looking at tombstones –

Clark: Yes?

Law: – are we looking at where the body –

Clark: You're looking at the head. Where the tombstone is, that's the head.

Law: Okay so actually the body's on the other side?

Clark: No, no. because if – depending on the side you're looking, the tombstone is always at the head of the casket.

Law: Okay but you take it the gravesite feet first, right?

Clark: Right.

Law: So how does – I'm trying to get –

Clark: When they place the headstones, it's at the head of the casket, on the person's head.

Law: All right.

Clark: The tombstone is not placed at the feet.

Law: Okay, I got it. Allright.

Clark: Somebody else's feet would be at somebody else's head.

Law: Okay. All right. I got it. I was having –

Clark: of that person is at the head of the casket.

Law: Okay. I got it. All right. I was having trouble –

Law: I was having trouble picturing that in my head.

Clark: One thing that I meant to tell you about this 8704 funeral – a full military funeral – that would also be with the caisson.

Law: Explain caisson to me.

Clark: The caisson is the horse-drawn caisson. You know like with Kennedy, with the horses.

Law: Does everybody get that?

Clark: No. No. That's a full military – those are just for the full military. Admiral and above.

Law: They get the caisson?

Clark: They get the caisson.

Law: Okay. All right. I got. So go back to your first day now and tell me –

Clark: So after doing all that, get it on to the grave site, folding the flag, just feeling a little nervous when they blew – I'm not really concerned about the fire hardly but when they blew…you get the – I got a chill. It was a little most like – it was like it went right through you.

Law: Right.

Clark: That sound [scat singing] and you're standing yourself when, "This is it. This is it for this person. It's over." When you get it, because saw a lot of meaning, you want to do the very best you can for this guy's family and for this individual who served his country, you wanted to be the best send off that this family ever had for this person.

Law: You're all very cognizant of that.

Clark: Excuse me.

Law: You're all very cognizant that you want to do the best job you can.

Clark: We want this to be the best funeral that it can be for this person. This is his final send off. And for the family, we want them to remember how sharp this was. When I say how sharp, about how great this was a send off of this person for their loved one.

Law: Now, this so I can keep track now, this is your first day on your first funeral-

Clark: This was my first funeral.

Law: – and the last funeral you did was John F. Kennedy.

Clark: John F. Kennedy, my very last. It's really, really – I didn't think of it but when I thought of it, I was like of all people that I've buried, this was like – When you think about it, Will, it's like, "Man, it gave." You could have left like a day before, you could have left like a week before, you could have left like a month before. And believe it or not, Will, I have received my orders already and I was slated to leave but the way it worked out Will,

I buried Kennedy the last day because the very next day, I shipped out. [laughs]

Law: Wow.

Clark: It's just yes, I know. I was like I don't know whether this is fate, I don't know whether – but this was my final day in the honor guard. And it was just amazing. And it wasn't like I had to stay an extra day or they kept me and – No, it just-

Law: It just fell that way.

Clark: Yes. And I don't mean to sound like airy but it just – I don't know. I remember the first person I buried and I remember the last person I buried.

Clark: But once I got that first one under my belt, I was ready. I just – I think I had like too more aware. I was at either on the head or the foot. And that the person that was in charge of the pallbearers, of all the pallbearers-

Law: What was his name?

Clark: He would tell me, he said, "You really did well today. You were sharp today."

Law: What was the – ?

Clark: Then I would add if, "When am I going to be on the head or when am I going to be on the foot?" Because they had more responsibility. And I knew, he knew I knew because I would show him when we were practicing. I could do it. I just – once I got on with that three of our carrion caskets, I just delved into it. I learned all the funerals. I learned what you're supposed to do, when you're supposed to do it. And I was there like four months and this guy, Harris, I believe his name was. Harris, he was getting ready to ship out. He was getting ready to ship out.

Law: This was the head of all the honor guard.

Clark: Right. He was the head of all the pallbearers, all four platoons and pallbearers.

Law: Okay.

Clark: Right?

Law: He was the head of your particular platoon.

Clark: No, no. He was the head of all the pallbearers-

Law: Okay.

Clark: – not just the first, second, third. He was in charge of all the pallbearers. He was in charge of training them. He was in charge of who he sent out, which platoon he sent out, who he wanted to do with the big funerals, he was in charge of it.

Clark: He'd invite the other petty officer.

Clark: I was in like four months and had lost all – any kind of fear or anything about going out. There were days when we would go out and we would have like four, five funerals in one day. We'd just be jumping from section to section toward funerals. Then we – they'd give us packed lunches. We eat packed lunches on the bus. We have like a half an hour, 45 minutes and then we head on next funeral. There were days where we'd be in on to cemetery with six to seven funerals. We were to have a funeral every like 35, 40 minutes, we would have a funeral.

Law: What kind of toll does it-

Clark: Sometimes, we got to do a funeral, jump on the bus, we race to another section of the carry out a funeral because I mean we would be in there all day sometimes.

Law: Now, just for my own clarification, when you're one of the pallbearers, it's not all Navy or it's not all Army or it's not all Marines, it's a mixture of –

Clark: No, no, no. No. Each branch of the military has their own pallbearers.

Law: Okay. So when you did fun –

Clark: The only time we would something to join is if it involved the president of the United States.

Law: Okay. So all of the people that you trained with were Navy guys.

Clark: Navy.

Law: Okay. What-

Clark: I didn't know Tim. I didn't know Bud. I didn't know Phil Bert, Mayfield, Gaudreau. I didn't know any of those guys. We've probably seen each other in Arlington because we would be crisscrossing. If I'll go from section to section, the Marines would be in one section, we'd be in another section, they already would be in another section. You'd be amazed at how many funerals would be going on and on in Arlington National Cemetery.

Law: What kind of toll does that take on a person day after day, after day, after day, sometimes funerals all day long, five funerals, seven funerals a day? What does that do to you psychologically?

Clark: Well, you got to understand that a lot of these guys were not young guys. These were not young men that were killed in battle. Every now and then, we would get a young guy. Sometimes, it would be a military child that has to be buried with their father or whoever at Arlington so you would have that. And that would make you feel you'd get sensitive today. But back in 1962, I can remember burying guys coming from Vietnam and we have never even heard of that place. But it's early as then, people would [sic] being buried in Arlington that were killed in Vietnam. And we have never heard of it. When you're that young people, we would see on the paper that they would give us: what section and who was being laid to rest. And you could see, 1944 or 1934 or from WWII or stuff like that. So a lot of them were older veterans that had passed away.

Law: Being young, you didn't give death much of a thought even though you were dealing with it every day?

Clark: No. I mean not becoming insensitive but It's like "I'm doing my job and I'm going to do it the best." But every funeral were invited is like a major thing for us. It was like the last send off for this person and we wanted to do the best job that we could to make the family feel that "Hey, these guys make me appreciate my spouse or my dad's military service."

Law: Do you remember the date that you first –

Clark: Went to Arlington?

Law: Yes. Went to Arlington. You remember the date?

Clark: Yes. It was in January and it was very cold.

Law: What was the year?

Clark: I don't remember the date but I know it was in January. It was cold.

Law: Was that 1962? The year?

Clark: No. 1963.

Law: So the first year that you set on Arlington Cemetery was 1963?

Clark: 1963. January of 1963. And I got to say there are not a lot of trees in Arlington. And those sections are like roaming hills. And when the wind whirls I'm telling you, you can almost be falling in the branch site. There are times that wind will be whipping and that flag and I mean we would really have to hold onto that flag because that flag would try and flap and if it gets away that is disrespectful. For us it is disrespectful. And then you are wearing white gloves and your hands are freezing but you endure. You just do what you need to do.

APPENDIX B

HSCA Interview With Richard Lipsey, 1-18-78

[NOTE: This transcript was created by Debra Conway of JFK Lancer Productions and Publications.]

Q: We are interviewing Richard A. Lipsey. The day is Jan 18, 1978. The time is appx. 20 of 12:00. We are in Baton Rouge, Louisiana at Steinberg's Sporting Goods Store. The business [tape unclear] of Richard Lipsey.

LIPSEY: That is correct. Now let me ask you fellows a question. Before we start and the only thing that I question about this conversation is that – and I don't even remember, I don't have a copy of it. Now, you know everything from getting the Honor Guard there and everything. And I did watch the autopsy, not all 100% of it but the majority of it. About a week or so later I remember signing a document that we that fell under some Federal Secrets Act, should not discuss any thing we felt was a secret nature particularly about the autopsy for 15 years. Now are you excluded from this?

Q: Well, it's our understanding…

LIPSEY: Not that I know anything that makes a hell of a lot of difference. We were just told not to discuss it and I don't remember if it is 15 years or 20 years. I definitely remember signing something of that nature.

Q: It's our position that we are pursuing this investigation pursuant to the mandate of Congress and that we hope you will wish to participate and give us the information in a voluntary manner.

LIPSEY: Fine. No question about it. As long as you feel that in your position with Congress that anything I may have signed would be null and voided as far as you are concerned.

Q: We are not in a position to give you legal advice as to what you should or should not do. It is our position that there will not be any harm coming to you for cooperating in our investigation because of what you tell us.

LIPSEY: I really don't think there is. I think the point of it was obviously until the investigation – this was when the investigation hadn't even started – was that really we didn't talk to reporters or anything until the investigation on the assassination of Pres. Kennedy was complete. I personally feel that was what it was. With that understanding, you know…

Q: If at any point you feel there is a particular item with a question of National Security, please consult with an attorney.

LIPSEY: I will. There's nothing that I can tell you that would have anything to do with National Security.

Q: Just for the record to clarify what the orders may have been, [tape unclear] were they orders to sign?

LIPSEY: I think it came through our Chief of Staff in our office. Military District of Washington. It came from our chief of staff, it was a Col. Holden. He got it from where ever. That's the best I can remember. Okay, let's go on from there.

Q: Preliminary we'd like you to state – we know your name already – your date of birth, and then also to go back to 1963 and what your general duties were, not just on that day, but in general as an aide to Gen Wehle.

LIPSEY: Born on Oct 7, 1939 in Selma, Alabama, and I reside right here in Baton Rouge. I was at the time, I'd been in the service I was stationed at Ft. Polk, Louisiana. While I was there several hundred Lt.'s got interviewed for the job, well didn't get interviewed, there were several hundred there, I was one of several that was fortunate enough to get interviewed for the job of aide de camp to Gen Wehle who was at Ft. Polk. I was selected as his Jr. aide at that time, I was a 2nd Lt.. Shortly thereafter, in June, Gen Wehle was notified that he was being transferred to Washington as commander general of MBW.

[Somewhat condensed for clarity] And his senior aide, as most Generals do, take care of their aides, arranged for senior aide to attend command and general staff college in Ft. Leavenworth, Kansas. And he asked me if I'd like to accompany him to Washington, which I did. I was very grateful to get out of Ft. Polk. When I got to Washington Gen. Wehle was due two aides, a senior, in his position, his aide could have been a Colonel or up to Captain. Gen Wehle and I got along very well. I had so much respect for him, he was just a super human being. We worked so well together that he just didn't get another aide, I was it. I took the place of both aides. So I was Gen Wehle's aide while he was the Commanding Secretary General in Washington. And also at some special events I served as a social aide at the White House, military aide at night at some occasions. But the majority of my time was spent working day and night for Gen Wehle.

Our duties basically – Gen W's duties, he was the senior military service in Washington, maybe not always in rank on some occasions, but he was the senior commanding General in Washington of a unit. And as such when all the services worked together – like the Army, Navy, Airforce,

Coast Guard, Marines – worked together on projects, receptions, when dignitaries came to the US on special events, on funerals, on parades, whatever, our service was the senior service and Gen Wehle was always in command. That's how we happened to handle the funeral obviously when Kennedy got killed. All ceremonial aspects of military, anything the military has to do with Washington in regard to ceremony, all the services participate, is run by the Army and since Gen Wehle was the commanding officer and I was his aide, I was the detail man. Did a lot of his planning and helped him a lot. The funeral was our project from the time I was in Washington and he was killed.

I happened to be driving up to the Gen's house at 1:00 to pick him up to go back to the office and had the radio on. And heard the news flash the same as everybody else did. The Gen had his radio on in the house and we met at the door. I was coming in as he was coming out. We immediately went back to our office and got on the phone with the White House. Got on the phone with the Pentagon, got on the phone with everybody else and immediately put what needed to be done into progress.

We met the body at Andrews Airforce Base. We had everything organized by that afternoon. We had Marines organized with their little Honor Guard. We had the men from Ft. Meyer, the third old [?] guard, the guys like at Humphry's funeral, the ceremonial guard that watched the casket. The ceremonial troop in Washington had been arranged to meet the body at Andrews. Put it in a hearse. We had a decoy hearse because we knew there was a mob waiting at Bethesda Naval Hospital. So we got in a couple of these helicopters with our honor guard when they left and flew over to the hospital to get there before they did. And when they came in, one of the hearses went right up to the front door. All of the crowd, of course, rushed over there. The one with the body in it went around to the back where the morgue was and we unloaded it. We met them in the back and unloaded it right there to avoid the news media and the crowd and everything else.

Q: The body was brought in the rear?

LIPSEY: The body was brought in the back door, backed right up to the loading ramp right immediately next to the morgue. And we unloaded it there and then Jackie Kennedy and her family and everybody that was, you know, flown to Washington and come back with the body, they came in the hospital the front way and went upstairs to the Presidential Suite at the hospital. Gen. Wehle went up to the suite to start to talk to Mrs. Kennedy to make the funeral arrangements with her, tentative arrangements mind you, because this was still early. Seeing what they wanted done and getting more wheels into motion because we didn't know exactly to do. And Gen Wehle told me, "Don't leave this body!" "You don't leave it," and I didn't except when he came back down and went in and spelled me for a little while.

Q: I have a question. How did you go from when Air Force One landed? How did you go from Andrews to Bethesda itself?

LIPSEY: We accompanied General Wehle in a helicopter.

Q: In a helicopter. While the body was being driven?

LIPSEY: Right.

Q: And then you were there when...

LIPSEY: The body was in the procession and going through Washington but there were two hearses and one pulled right up to the front door and one went around with the body, went around to the back of the hospital.

Q: Were you present when the body was taken out of, to the rear?

LIPSEY: I was standing there at the airplane when it was loaded into the hearse and then I was standing right there. I helped then unload the casket myself when we were at the hospital. Right.

Q: And then you accompanied it from that point on?

LIPSEY: Then never left it.

Q: You stayed with the body?

LIPSEY: Right.

Q: Okay, I guess we can go on.

LIPSEY: It's up to you to start asking questions now.

Q: You just go on...

LIPSEY: Remember this is 14 years ago. I mean it's so little span of time and I've thought about it so often recounted it to friends all except for what I actually saw at the autopsy. We took the body to the morgue. The only other person that I can remember besides the doctors, and there were the team of doctors that worked on the body, the only other person that I can remember, beside the doctors was inside of the room was a 1st Lt. Sam Bird. I was a 1st Lt. Sam was head of the Old Guard, I really can't think of what they called them, the guys, two or three teams of fellows that were always responsible of the casket in a ceremony – when a general died. Three of them march on each side of the casket, enlisted men and there is an officer in charge. At all the important funerals held while I was there, Sam was always the officer in charge. He was the guy that had been standing there all night long ready to pick up the casket or do whatever's necessary and move it around. He was in charge of the detail that guarded the casket, a formality-type thing. He was there, in and out of the room during the autopsy.

So, anyhow. They brought the body in, took it out. Laid it on the table. It was the first dead man I'd ever seen, and I'd never seen an autopsy, obviously, I'd never seen an autopsy before. So it was a pretty traumatic experience. I wouldn't really, quite frankly, I couldn't tell the General, "No, I not going in the room." So I went. I'd never realized seeing a dead man with rigor mortis – it just didn't seem like you were looking at a dead person, it was just entirely a different thing. It didn't bother me at all. I remember that Sam went out during the ceremony and sent one of his men to get us some hamburgers, it was late at night since we hadn't eaten since that morning. We sat in there watching part of the autopsy eating hamburgers. So obviously there was the smell of formaldehyde in there. That's what bothered me. The smell was worse than the sight.

So, we watched the autopsy. Once again, my hours are a little fuzzy. The autopsy lasted approx. , if I'm not mistaken, approx. 3 – 4 hours. After that we stayed in the room. When the men from the funeral home came in, because, by this time when Gen Wehle had come back down, but he was in and out. He was still making a lot of arrangements, but he would come in occasionally for a couple of minutes to let me go out and take a little break. Then the men from the funeral home came in and we sat there while they more or less put him back together and made the cosmetic, made the different cosmetic changes that had to be made on the body.

By that time I had sent my car to the White House to get some clothes for Kennedy and they'd come back. They'd called the White House and told them.

Q: Who is "they?" The company that drove … ?

LIPSEY: Gen Wehle got someone from the Kennedy family to call the White House to tell them what clothes. We sent our driver Gen had a permanent car and chauffeur. I sent my driver to the White House and got …

Q: Did he take anyone with him, maybe a presidential aide? Agent? Anyone else?

LIPSEY: I honestly couldn't tell you. I have no earthly idea. All I know is the got the clothes from the White House and I helped the funeral home. By that time, by then I think there were only two of them in the room. I helped them dress him, helped them pick up the body, [helped them] dress him. I helped them pick him up and laid him in the casket. And as far as I know I was the last to look at him – standing there when they closed it. Then the story just goes on and on about the funeral. I don't know how really relevant that part can be. Just formal planning and carrying out the funeral.

Q: Getting back to the beginning stages of the autopsy, or even before the actual autopsy began, do you recall when the x-rays were taken, the x-rays and photos?

LIPSEY: Yeah, well as far as the exact x-rays were taken, no I don't recall. I do recall the comments from the doctors, you know, who started examining the body before they did anything, you know, looking at the body, looking at where the bullets had entered the back of the his head. It was obvious that one bullet entered the back of his head and exited on the right side of his face and pretty well blew away the right side of his head. And then the other two bullets had entered the lower part of his neck and the best of my knowledge, or the best of my memory, one had exited. The other bullet had entered from behind and hit his chest cavity and the bullet went down into the body. And during the autopsy, this is the only part that I can imagine would be of any – really, what I've told you right there, of strictly confidential nature that was never written up anywhere. And I presume, am I right, that this tape and this conversation is strictly confidential? You know, it's not going to be published I guess is what I'm getting at?

Q: It's not going to be published during the term of this committee. During 1978.

LIPSEY: Okay, Well, is that as far as I can remember, and I'm pretty positive about it, they never found that third bullet. It did not exit the body. When they did the autopsy first they cut the top of his head off and then they cut his chest open, you know, and they got all of his insides out, that was the only gory part, they took them out a piece at a time and laid them up on, I remember, a beautiful clean stainless steel rack with water pouring over it all the time. I imagine to keep it fresh or whatever. They did the whole autopsy then they came back and, you know, sliced up all the organs.

Q: For slides?

LIPSEY: I don't know what they were using them for. They were taking pictures of them, they, you know, and they were examining them. I don't know whether they were taking them for records or not. I don't think the doctors, to be perfectly frank, I don't think it ever entered the doctors' minds that they were taking pictures for a formal investigation. They were doing an autopsy, a complete autopsy, and whatever physical records that you maintain during an autopsy was what they were doing. I know they did a very thorough job because every time one to them would say something the other one would question it. I can remember they looked at this one organ and they passed it around and all three discussed it before they would go on to the most part. You know, it wasn't one guy doing his operating on the feet, one on the chest, and one on the head. They did everything together and re-examined everything together. I remember that distinctly. They looked like one of the most efficient teams doing anything that I've ever seen. But anyhow, like I say. I can remember lifting his chest cavity and then the top of his head off, and you know, all the internal organs out. And I can remember them discussing the third, third bullet. First, second and third bullet. The third bullet, the one they hadn't found. Their only logical explanation was that it hit him in the back of the head, hit his chest cavity and then, like bullets will do – I am sure you are familiar with that one, you could shoot somebody, no telling where the bullet is going to and up – probably hit his chest cavity and could have gone all the way down into his toe. You know, it could have just hit and gone right down into his leg or wherever. But I don't think, to the best of my knowledge, they ever found the third bullet.

Q: Did they find any other bullets?

LIPSEY: This is what I'm getting back to. I don't know that they found bullets or whether they found just particles of bullets. I don't think they know. I don't think they found any whole bullets. But that is just strictly speculation on my part. I remember they were bound and determined to find that bullet because it didn't have an exit mark. But I don't think they ever found the bullet. The one that hit his chest, the one that exited here – [corrects himself] entered here; there was no exit hole. So the bullet was somewhere in his body, obviously.

Q: When you say "entered here" referring to?

LIPSEY: The lower back of the neck.

Q: Lower back.

LIPSEY: From the angle they were talking about it had to come from quite a height because they were looking and talking to each other the angle they were pointing that had hit him had to be a down angle. Also all of them, their entire discussion – I never entered the discussion and neither did Sam Bird. We were sitting there watching and listening. And we weren't asked our opinion, for obvious reasons. We wouldn't have known what we were talking about. We never entered in any conversation with the docs or offered any information except when we were talking.

And I didn't personally think, personal opinion, from listening to the doctors, watching the autopsy, there was no question in their minds that the bullets came from the same direction that all three bullets came from the same place at the same time. They weren't different angles. They all had the same pattern to them.

Q: Okay, getting back to the bullets themselves, not the bullets themselves but the entrances, can you just go over again the entrances as you remember them?

LIPSEY: Alright, as I remember them there was one bullet that went in the back of the head that exited and blew away part of his face. And that was sort of high up, not high up but like this little crown on the back of your head right there, three or four inches above your neck. And then the other one entered at more of less the top of the neck, the other one entered more of less at the bottom of the neck.

Q: Okay, so that would be up where the crown, not the top of the head?

LIPSEY: Yeah, the rear crown.

Q: Where that point might be on the skull bone?

LIPSEY: Exactly.

Q: Then one approximately several inches lower?

LIPSEY: Well not several but two or three inches lower.

Q: Still in the head? Or what we would call …

LIPSEY: Closer to the neck.

Q: Closer to the neck? And than one in the neck?

LIPSEY: In the lower neck region.

Q: In the back?

LIPSEY: Yeah, the very – right as the ….

Q: Let's go back over things. Sometimes visual aids you forget. Okay, and then according to the autopsy doctors they feel the one that entered in the skull, in the rear of the head, exited the right side of the head?

LIPSEY: The right front, you know, the face. Not the right top, the right front. The facial part of your face. In other words...

Q: Did that destroy his face at all? You say Presidents Kennedy, was his face distorted?

LIPSEY: Yeah, the right side. If you looked at him straight. If you looked at him from the left you couldn't see anything. If you looked at him from the right side it was just physically part of it blown away.

Q: So that would be right here?

LIPSEY: Yeah, behind the eye and everything.

Q: Behind the eye? Was it all hair region or was it part of the actual face?

LIPSEY: To the best of my recollection it was part of the hair region and part of the face region.

Q: Just to follow up this point, after the embalming had been done and the morticians finished preparing the body and you viewed President Kennedy at that time, after he was dressed, could you see any damage?

LIPSEY: They did a beautiful job. He looked great.

Q: So you really couldn't tell?

LIPSEY: Oh, you could tell, sure, if you got up close you could tell, yes.

Q: But he was presentable in the sense that you....

LIPSEY: He wasn't presentable in the sense that you would want to open the casket. But they did a super job.

Q: What I guess I'm getting at is half his face so completely blown away? Could you recognize him?

LIPSEY: No, not at all. Oh no, he was 100% recognizable. I mean, particularly after they finished. No, it wasn't that much damage at all.

Q: Now getting back, we just went over the three entrances and what the doctor's stated were entrances. To refresh your memory, the first doctor was Dr. Humes... is the chief pathologist...

LIPSEY: [Talking over questioner] I met the doctors when it first started except when I read their names – I don't know them then; I don't know them now – on a personal basis. Nor I never talked to them before, during or afterwards.

Q: You do recollect Commander Humes?

LIPSEY: Yes. Okay, the only thing I remember there at times was another, it wasn't a doctor. It could have been a doctor. I know there was an assistant or an aide doing things for them during different periods.

Q: Getting back to the entrances you just stated one exit you believed was on the right hand side of the head. Now what about the other entrances, what about the corresponding exits if there were any? Let's clarify that a little more. For starting, one...

LIPSEY: The bullet entered lower part of the head or upper part of the neck. [long pause] To the best of my knowledge, came out the front of the neck. But the one that I remember they spent so much time on, obviously, was the one they found did not come out. There was a bullet – that's my vivid recollection cause that's all they talked about. For about two hours all they talked about was finding that bullet. To the rest of my recollection they found some particles but they never found the bullet – pieces of it, trances of it. The best of my knowledge, this is one thing I definitely remember they just never found that whole bullet.

Q: What was it you observed that made you feel that exited – the bullet that entered the rear portion of his head exited in the throat area?

LIPSEY: The throat area. Right. The lower throat area.

Q: What, were there markings there that indicated that the doctors came to that conclusion?

LIPSEY: I saw where, you know, they were working and also listening to their conclusions.

Q: And it's your recollection at that time was that the doctors definitely felt the bullets came from the one area, same area, same time?

LIPSEY: Yes, they talked about that. It never seemed to be any doubt in their mind the bullets were coming from different directions at all.

Q: It's been a long time but do you recall any reasons they gave?

LIPSEY: Because of the angle. I remember that's how they kept talking bout the angles of the bullets because the angles that they entered the body. That's why, they, I remember, measuring and doing all kinds of things. They turned the body up at one point to determine where that bullet that entered back here that didn't have an exit mark. Where was that bullet? And so when it got to down to where they thought it hit his chest cavity, they opened him up and started looking in here. That's why I remember one thing, they took, after they had taken all his organs out, during the autopsy they had them sitting up there: "Now let's see if we can find the bullet." They cut all his organs apart. I don't know what they did with them, I don't remember but they put them in some kind of containers. I don't remember but they put them in containers.

Q: Okay. One of the tapes stopped. Mr. Lipsey is also taping this interview and his taped stopped. 12:07 starting again.

Q: Getting back again to the beginning of the autopsy I think we can follow through on and answer some questions. Do you recall what time the photographs were taken?

LIPSEY: I remember them, and there again, that's [tape skips] I remember them taking the photographs but I don't remember what time. I have no idea.

Q: Do you know what they did with the photographs?

LIPSEY: I wasn't concerned about them. Never entered my mind to even ask. I might point out at this time that Sam Bird, the other Lt. that I'm talking about. And I could kick myself 3 times for not doing it. We had a lot of documented records that had to do with the funeral itself. You know, planning it and the Old Guard, the presidents, and the kings and queens who all were there. Every step of the record. I've got a lot of those records at home, newspapers with my picture on the cover during the funeral and all that.

But I do remember, right after, this was all started Friday night and we buried him on Monday afternoon. I remember Tuesday night or Wednesday night, one night that week, sitting in Sam's apartment. He made a recording on the everything he had seen and done from the time Kennedy was assassinated until the time they buried him, for his own personal record. And I could kick my self for not doing the same thing. But I remember him doing that.

Q: This was on the Tuesday or Wednesday night?

LIPSEY: Tuesday, Wednesday night after the autopsy. The autopsy was Friday night. I remember we left after the autopsy. I was sitting there with Sam. the funeral people put Kennedy back together. That took almost as long as the autopsy. It was sometime in the very early hours of the morning. I've got that documented at home. I guess it was sometime between 3 and 4 in the morning. We finally finished and we put the body back into the hearse. And Jackie Kennedy came down and got into the hearse with the body herself. Still had on the pink suit – she hadn't changed clothes.

We led it. Gen Wehle and myself were the first car. If I'm not mistaken, there was a police car in front of us. The hearse right behind us. Then a family car behind that. One or two other cars in the procession. We went back to the White House. We drove up, went into the White House, parked. We'd had all this arranged so it had to be very formalized now. Mrs. K and the hearse with the body stopped at the entrance. We called, I'll never forget this, we called the Marine barracks which was across the river in Virginia twenty minutes before we left the hospital. It might have been 15 minutes, we called them and told them we wanted an honor guard to lead the body into the White House and to make a cordon as the Old Guard moved and carried it out of the White House. [seems very moved, voice tight with grief]

They woke those boys out of a dead sleep and they were at the White House before we were. They had a group of them marching in front of the hearse. Went very slow. We took the body out, took it in the white house. Into the East Room if I remember correctly. At that time they had a priest there. It was Bobby, Jackie, White House servants, one or two other people and Gen Wehle and myself. They had a little private service, a little Funeral service lasting 10-15 minutes. That picture ended up a double page spread. They ended up they had a photographer in there. No other news service allowed there. It must have been an official photograph. That ended up as a double page spread picture in a magazine. That doesn't have anything to do with what you're trying to find out.

Q: Do you remember whether Sam Bird discussed the details of the autopsy on the tape?

LIPSEY: No I don't' I remember him making the tape. I remember asking me questions about who was there in order to authenticate. As far as I remember when I came into his room he had been making the tape. I was not present when he discussed the autopsy part on the tape. I'm not sure he put it on tape. But I know for a fact that he made a tape recording of his part in the whole thing. To that point, if he did put it on tape, about the autopsy and basically we saw the exact same thing, that tape would be a lot more valuable to you than what I am telling you today. It would be a lot more valuable.

Q: Is Sam Bird still alive today? Have you talked to him?

LIPSEY: I haven't talked to Sam since the day I left Washington. I left Washington in around this time in 1074.

Q: Was he still stationed there?

LIPSEY: Yeah. He was still stationed there when I left. I imagine he stayed there for his tour of duty. Matter of fact, Gen Wehle asked Sam – Sam and I got to be very good friends. We lived right across from each other at Ft. Meters in the Officer's HQ. Sam had he had been a general's aide at his previous station. When I left Washington Gen W got me to ask Sam if he would replace me as Gen Wehle's aide. Sam felt he'd been a general's aide once and he felt he needed a tour of duty on his records instead of another general aide position just so he could seek rank faster. I don't know if he stayed in the Army or got out of the Army. He was a permanent type. To the best of my knowledge Sam Bird's probably still in the Army, if he's alive. And I certainly hope he is. He was a fine person.

Q: In the early stages of the autopsy before they formally began cutting, who was running things?

LIPSEY: I can't tell you. There were doctors in there. One doctor was obviously directing the procedures. I don't know which one it was.

Q: Was the doctor directing the procedures one of the participating in the autopsy?

LIPSEY: Yes.

Q: Did the autopsy surgeons discuss among themselves what type of autopsy they would do?

LIPSEY: Not during the autopsy, no.

Q: Do you remember any discussions prior to the autopsy?

LIPSEY: I wasn't with them prior to the autopsy. They were there when we got there

Q: From the time that you arrived, until they were into the autopsy, do you remember the doctors discussing the nature of the autopsy?

LIPSEY: I'm sure they must have. No. I'm not sure they must have. They must have discussed it among themselves. Whether they discussed with anybody else or the chief of surgery of the hospital. I'm sure they probably did. I don't know. I honestly don't know. I can't make any comment on that because I don't know.

Q: Did they have any discussions with anyone else during the autopsy?

LIPSEY: No. Not to my knowledge.

Q: Were you in the positions to be able to hear any conversations among the doctors?

LIPSEY: Yeah, I was, but truthfully, I paid attention to what I wanted to pay attention to. It was one of those deals where I was curious how many times he'd been shot, or where he'd been shot. Medical definitions of what type of wounds they were, and whatever, I tuned all that out probably. I didn't know what they were talking about and I just didn't care. I should have cared more – I wish now I could have taped it, if possible.

No. I really don't know… I heard their conversations. I was interested in the parts I wanted to be interested in. It's been too long to recall the other parts of their conversations.

Q: I'd like to stop the tape in order to change sides. The time is 12:17.

•••••

Time is 12:18 beginning the tape again.

Q: Getting back to the question that he just asked you. In terms of feet, how close were you to the table where the autopsy was being performed? Were you right behind?

LIPSEY: When you walked in the autopsy room from the back door where they brought the body in, you turned left down a very little short hallway. Had the doors right there. When you walked in there was sort of a like a little spectator's gallery, on the right there were several chairs on the right with a railing in front. The table was in front of that. I would say I was about as far as from that jacket, maybe, from the doctors, approximately about 12-15 feet.

They did make a comment when they laid him on the table or anything that has nothing to do with anything. He was a beautiful physical specimen. He had not an ounce of fat his body anywhere, very muscular. Great looking physical shape. Obviously he looked like a dead person.

But, he looked smaller, I saw him quite a bit and he looked much smaller. Just his physical condition was fantastic – not fat or any sloppiness anywhere.

Q: When the autopsy doctors first walked up to the table, did they did they thoroughly look over the body or did they concentrate on one area and begin to work there.

LIPSEY: The first thing they did was look over the body. I can remember that, you know, from head to toe, all sides. They just looked at the whole thing. And made, they discussed a lot of things. That's probably the part I tuned out. I do remember looking it over thoroughly. I do remember the body still was covered with blood. I remember them cleaning it off, taking, I remember a brush, a scrub brush, cleaning the body in certain areas before they started cutting. I remember after they finished, scrubbing it down again, you know, getting all the mess away and everything. They scrubbed and cleaned it pretty good after all the preliminary looking they wanted to, before they physically touched the body, they had to clean the body before they started.

Q: Did the doctors in that preliminary examination find all the wounds you have described?

LIPSEY: I'm sure they must have. They were visible.

Q: To follow that up, the wounds that you describe, was that based on hearing the doctors calling out that this is a wound, this is a wound? Or was that based on your visible sight when you saw the body?

LIPSEY: Both. Because, I could see the body, I could see the rear. I could see obviously the side of the face. Although that's just when I walked in they took him out the casket – I saw that. Beside the side wound, because when I went back and sat down, they laid him down to right. The way they laid him I was looking at the left side of his body as opposed to the right side of his body. I remember I could see the blood at the throat area, and in the neck area. As for as me getting down and looking at the exit hole in the front, all I could see was the blood. What I'm talking about is what I heard in conversation from them, from then on.

Q: To follow that up, as you should well know because I take it you do hunt a lot, locating wounds in hair is very difficult. The sighting. Did you visibly see the wounds in the back of the head, what you feel were the entrance wounds? Was based on what the doctors stated that we know their opinions ...

[Lipsey is interrupting with "No... That's ... No."]

LIPSEY: No. That's...No. I hope I'm not contradicting myself. But at this point, there again, like I said, it's been a long time. I feel that there was no really entrance wound – maybe I said that – in the rear of his head. There was a point where they determined the bullet entered the back of his head but I believe all of that part of his head was blown. I mean I think it just physically blew away that part of his head. You know, just like a strip right across there or may have been just in that area – just blew it out..

Q: So you say the damage caused by the entrance and the exit of the bullet to the head caused one large hole?

LIPSEY: To the best of my recollection, yes it did. But one, the other one went in the back of the neck. Like a say, I saw the blood spots and what have you, but they weren't tremendous, not a blow-a-way like this. But, of course, what little I know about it, which isn't a hell of a lot, your bone is right there, so when it hit it, the bullet probably expanded, hit something solid and ripped. But here, it went in to tissue before it hit anything.

Q: Was there any discussion of the nature of the bullet which caused the head wound?

LIPSEY: No. To my recollection, no there wasn't.

Q: Was there any discussion that it would take a certain kind of bullet to cause that kind of damage?

LIPSEY: If it was done, it was probably, I'm thinking, it was probably done in the privacy of the doctors after the autopsy. I don't remember – and I'm sure it must have been mentioned during the autopsy but I'm not going to say yes or no because I don't have any idea. I don't remember that at all.

Q: During the autopsy, did you discuss with anyone else in the room the nature of head wounds. Or the causes of them?

LIPSEY: No. Not really. Sam and I ...We just talked about different things. We talked about Kennedy, talked about how many times he had been shot. I don't think we ever discussed anything in relation to what the doctors were saying about the wounds.

Q: Could you describe for us the nature of the damage to the front of the neck?

LIPSEY: No. I really couldn't. Because like I say, when we got it out, there was – blood was all over the body. It was almost caked on. I remember they took a scrub brush and a pail. One of his arms, and if I've not mistaken, it was his left arm. You know, the way, I guess, after he died, finished the autopsy by that time and, rigor mortis had set in and one of his arms was slightly higher. Well, the guy's laying down and one of them was up a little bit. So when they started the autopsy I can remember, one of the doctors, when he was starting to clean the body up, got up on the table and physically got up on the table and put his knee down on his arm to hold it down – to get it out of his way – so he could scrub the rest of the body. So to say, to describe the hole to you, no. Because it was so messy and so much blood that I didn't, I never got close enough to get down and look at the wound itself.

Q Can you give us an rough estimate, compared it for example to the wound in the head and the wound in the back ...

LIPSEY: It was much smaller, very much smaller.

Q: ... Than the head wound ...

LIPSEY: Than the side head wound.

Q: What about the wound on the back?

LIPSEY: There again the wound in the back of the head, all I saw of that wound was when they turned him on his side. And saw the blood when they were cleaning him off, cutting, and doing the thing. I couldn't possibly describe to you the relation to the size. I don't' remember and I doubt that I saw it close enough to describe it to you.

Q: Do you remember whether the doctors describing the wound in the neck as being caused by anything other than a bullet?

LIPSEY: No.

Q: Do you remember discussions on whether or not there was a tracheotomy incision?

LIPSEY: [Long Pause.] No. I guess anything I do remember something about that – I remember it would have to come after reading about what went on in Dallas. I just don't remember discussing that.

Q: What have you read about Dallas? About that front neck wound?

LIPSEY: It's been so long. Like I say, I'm glad I hadn't. I'm glad I didn't go back over any articles and read because I don't even remember.

Q: You don't recall whether there was a tracheotomy in the front of the neck?

LIPSEY: Absolutely not.

Q: Well, you say you didn't you hear the doctors discuss that. Did you explicitly hear the doctors say that the wound in the front of the neck was caused by a bullet?

LIPSEY: If you want to get down to specifics: no. The only thing I do remember was when they kept talking about the entrance in the back of the neck and looking at the hole in the front of the neck. To the best of my knowledge they were convinced that a bullet came out the front of the neck. And that's how they were determining where to look for the other bullet – by the angle it went in at the back and came out at the front. Where to look at the other one.

Q: Oh, the angle where it came in the head – looking out the front of the neck – using that angle…

LIPSEY: Right. Right. [Interrupting] To determine where to look for the other one, I presume from what they were looking at, both entrances looked to be the same.. In other words, both entrances – the angles were the same were on both entrances, or the sizes of the holes probably was the same – and in the front. I'm not going to stand here and make up a story, make it sound good, I just don't remember whether they discussed the size of a trach hole or it in relation to where a bullet might have exited.

Q: How much time would you say, relatively speaking, did the doctors spent on the 3 wounds you described? Did they spend more time on one or the other of the wounds?

LIPSEY: They spent more time looking for that other bullet than they did on anything else.

Q: You're describing the bullet that went in…

LIPSEY: …on the lower part of the neck. I remember them saying it must of hit the chest cavity and ricocheted down somewhere into the body.

Q: Do you remember any discussion…

LIPSEY: And they spent a lot of time on that. Because I remember when they cut him open in the front, you know, they – I remember – "Let's look for this, let's look for this." They took all the organs out, they went through, they cut the organs up looking for bullets. And finally, to the best of my knowledge, and I remember this, I don't remember how much more they did after this, but I remember them saying: "That bullet could be anywhere." It could have gone right down to his heels or his toes. It could have ricocheted and traveled right down through right on down, you know, through his insides.

Q: Do you remember any discussion among the doctors that the bullet could have entered lower in the neck – lower back part of the neck exited in the front of the neck?

LIPSEY: Yeah. I remember they were firmly convinced it did not.

Q: Okay. So you're convinced…

LIPSEY: That's why they spent so much time looking for it. They traced it through the back of his neck through, you know, when they did the autopsy, through the inside of his body and there was no where the bullet was then where it should have exited, it was not. And at the angle it was traveling, and from, you know, with the other things they saw visible in the chest area once they cut him open, you know, it had started down, but where was it?

Q: When they opened up the body from the front, did – were they able to discern any part of the track of the bullet?

LIPSEY: I'm convinced they were in the upper part of his body – yes – because that's how they started following it. And then I think, that's when they started taking his organs out, you know, one at a time only. They took all of the insides out, I remember that, boy. They had four or five piles of insides sitting on the table. And they thoroughly examined each one of those. They just had a big hollow chest and stomach cavity left – or particularly chest cavity, when they got through. And, I'm very convinced, in my own mind, that they were very convinced that bullet was somewhere in him.

Because, from their conversations, they tracked this bullet as far as they could in a downward position before they couldn't tell where it went. That's when they started taking organs apart and looking where ever they could look without going ahead and just cutting him apart. And I think their decision finally was, we're just, you know, not going to completely dissect him to find this bullet. So they tracked the bullet down as far as it went. Obviously, by that point it wasn't that important.

Q: When they opened up the chest, when you say they saw part of the track of the bullet, did they take a photograph of that?

LIPSEY: Can't tell. I honestly do not know.

Q: Let me ask you this: Did they take all the photographs at the beginning or did they take some during the course of the autopsy?

LIPSEY: [Long pause] Once again, I don't know. I just don't know.

Q: Do you remember, you expressed, that you said the doctors considered the possibility that the bullet could be virtually anywhere in the body, including, I think the word you mentioned was "as far as the heel" Do you remember whether or not the doctors x-rayed...

LIPSEY: I remember one of the doctors said I've seen a guy shot – something to the effect, "I've seen bullet wounds hit bone and ricocheted all over the body." And he says, "We may never find this bullet unless we take the whole body apart."

Q: Do you remember whether they x-rayed the lower extremities?

LIPSEY: No, I don't.

Q: Do you recall if they were using x-rays at the same time they were dissecting?

LIPSEY: No.

Q: Do you remember the doctors looking at the x-rays during the autopsy room?

LIPSEY: That I do. I remember looking at them. That must have been… You're jogging my memory now because I do remember them looking at x-rays at the beginning of the autopsy, so they must have taken some at the at very beginning because I remember them relating x-rays to things they were doing.

Q: Do you remember which portion of the X-rays…

LIPSEY: No, no, no, no. I plead dumbness on that, I just don't… But I remember now, them holding [mumbling] things, this long thing in series with lights. They'd examine part of an x-ray and go on from there. So, obviously, they must have taken x-rays right at the beginning. If they took any more during or after, I don't remember.

Q: Do you remember any of the autopsy doctors arriving at the autopsy later than the others?

LIPSEY: No, I don't.

Q: Do you remember any of the autopsy doctors probing any of the wounds?

LIPSEY: Not, no, I really can't say. They were doing everything so I don't… I can say they must have, I'm not going to say they did. I remember, the wounds, looking for the bullet, were their primary concern.

[Interruption by intercom]

Q: Do you remember any discussion when they were trying to find out where the bullet went – of the possibility that the bullet had gone in the back and had fallen out of the body? In other words, a non-exited bullet remained in…

LIPSEY: [Interrupts] No. There was no possibility, there were no other holes it could have fallen out.

Q: That's what I mean – Did they discuss…

LIPSEY: [Interrupts] …to the rear. In other words…

Q: [Talking over Lipsey] That's what I mean. Fell out of the entrance.

LIPSEY: The bullet has penetrated. It went into his skin. There was evidence of it inside his body. It had penetrated the body. There was no way it could have fallen out.

Q: Was there any discussion because of external cardiac massage from the front when he was face up it could have fallen out?

LIPSEY: No. There was no discussion of that that I recall.

Q: Do you recall any phone calls anyone in the autopsy room made?

LIPSEY: In the room you mean?

Q: Anyone from the room or anyone from the room leaving the room to make a call?

LIPSEY: I made a call.

Q: From the room?

LIPSEY: No. Not from the room, but when the autopsy was over, before the men from the funeral home started their work, they took a break. Gen Wehle came in and asked if I wanted to go out for a while. Gen Wehle came into the room and I went out of the room and took 10 or 15 minutes. And called my parents and said, "Guess where I am or what I just did?" Woke them up, it was then after 2:00 in the morning. They said, "What?" "I just watched Kennedy's autopsy." Yes, we saw you on television this afternoon at Andrews Airforce Base and all that. I'll participate to a much greater extent at the funeral. Watch television – you'll see me. Typical, you know, I guess, 21 year old's reaction. That was the sum total of my reaction to my parents. I didn't discuss anything about anything. Just, I've been watching the autopsy. If anybody else called ... I don't know.

Q: Do you remember any messages being sent into the room by the Kennedy family or anybody with the Kennedy's?

LIPSEY: No.

Q: Do you remember Adm. Burkeley being in present at the autopsy?

LIPSEY: Everybody, to my knowledge, in that room besides Sam Bird and myself had on a medical gown. And so, if he was,

Q: [Interrupted] Just a minute. The time is now 12:38, Lipsey's tape ran out. [changing tape noises for a few minutes]

LIPSEY: If there was anybody – 20 minutes to 1:00, I'm starting again. If there was anybody else in the room, Admiral or who, he was dressed as a doctor and not as an officer, that I can recollect. I don't remember if he was in the room or not. No, I don't.

Q: Do you know who Admiral Burkeley is or was at the time?

LIPSEY: I don't remember his name.

Q: Do you remember meeting the physician of the President?

LIPSEY: No. I don't think I ever did.

Q: Who else do you remember was in the room?

LIPSEY: I can remember, like I say, if he was a doctor or an orderly. Other people at particular times cleaned the body, moved the body. Certain things like that. Occasionally somebody would just come into the room, turn around and walk out, one of the hospital staff-type people. But I don't remember who it was. I don't remember, by name, anybody else in the room.

Q: Do you recall anyone else who seemed to be filling the role of you were, observer, but not actually involved in assisting the doctors in any capacity?

LIPSEY: You know that's hard because I seem to recollect one other person in there on occasion, but for the life of me, honestly, I just can't remember who it was. I really don't. Sam and I were sitting to try to be out of the doctor's way and everybody else's way. Immediately away from the table but right there in the chairs as you walk in on the right. I just don't remember the other people who came in around at that time.

Q: Were you in charge of security arrangements for the autopsy room?

LIPSEY: Specifically, no. I was charged by Gen Wehle to make sure that no body left – that body didn't go anywhere without him or me. As far as specific security of the room on the outside, I remember they had guards all up and down that place. And Army people and all types of security people. And I don't know who physically was responsible for hospital security.

Q: Do you remember what orders, if any, on who could be admitted to the autopsy room?

LIPSEY: No, I probably wasn't around to be admitted. I had on my uniform and the Gen's recognition, and the Gen and I drove and everyone realized that he was in charge. He told me to stay with the body and from then on nobody ever asked me anything. But, there was a guard right outside the door. A policeman, a Washington policeman right outside the door.

Q: Do you remember anyone in effect taking attendance of who was present, circulating a list?

LIPSEY: No, I do not. Now I'm not going to say they didn't, but I don't remember.

Q: Getting back to the organs, you say they removed the organs the from the body and placed them up on the table – a stainless steel table...

LIPSEY: [Interrupting] It was right over the body.

Q: Shelving.

LIPSEY: Just shelving right over the body. And I remember it had water draining over it continuously.

Q: Now you also mentioned they examined these closely and also cut them up to some degree. Did they return some of them organs or all the organs to the body at the termination of the autopsy or do you recollect…?

LIPSEY: To the best of my knowledge, they didn't return any thing to the body. They had these organs in separate containers. After they examined them. What they did – I left for a while when Gen. Wehle came in to spell me – and when I went back we started working on – not we – a few people started to cleaning him up, cosmetically fixing him up. I don't remember what happened to his organs.

Q: Specifically, do you recall the brain being a part of these organs?

LIPSEY: I remember them cutting the top of his head off. I remember taking, I could see them taking everything out. That was the only point in the autopsy that I got a little queasy. I remember they made a little circular cut and started taking the things out from inside of his head.

Q: Do you remember what they put the brain in?

LIPSEY: No, I don't.

Q: Do you remember them taking any metal fragments out of the president's body?

LIPSEY: Specifically, no, I don't.

Q: Do you recall if they did take out any metal fragments, maybe you don't specifically remember where. Did they take any fragments at all?

LIPSEY: I would hope Sam could remember and put those down on his tape. I feel like they did, but I'm not going to sit here and say what part of the body they took them from or what they were. I feel like they had did have some bullet fragments. I remember them very carefully examining the area, around the part on the side of his head where it was kinda blown away. I remember just very extremely carefully examining that part of his head and looking for things. But I not going to tell you that they took a big piece or little piece out. Sorry, I just don't remember.

Q: I have a sketch here from the autopsy face sheet we'd like you to place, you can do it in pencil first and then in pen or just in pen, any wounds you recall.

LIPSEY: okay

Q: This sketch is a blank drawing of a body, a male body.

LIPSEY: Like I said, to the best of my knowledge somewhere in that area and in that area.

Q: Could you label them as of whether they are of entrance or of exit?

LIPSEY: Alright. [writing and speaking] Part blown away. Entrance and entrance. To the best of my... let's see it would be the right side of his face. That area in there. Once again, that area was kind of blown away.

Q: Is that area the same area?

LIPSEY: Same area. And there was a hole – you're talking about at tracheotomy. As far as I remember they were talking about it being a bullet hole. [writing and speaking] Exit. Exit.

Q: Could you put the date and your signature?

Q: Do you recall anyone in the room taking notes?

LIPSEY: Not around us, no. I do recall the doctors had like a chart sheet, like a clipboard with papers on it, making notes as they went along.

Q: Do you remember the presence of any federal agents in the room?

LIPSEY: No, I don't.

Q: When did you finish your duties as?

LIPSEY: Excuse me, there was one other person. Like I say, I'm just trying to remember. To the best of my recollections everybody was dressed in a surgical gown around the table but there may have been one other person whether it was the admiral, chief surgeon, or a federal agent, there was another person around the table at times that wasn't doing anything, was observing. He could have been one of the doctors. I do remember another person. I couldn't tell you any more about it.

Q: When did your service as Gen Wehle's aide end?

LIPSEY: When I got out of the service, which was January of '74.

Q: Did you help make the arrangements for the re-interment of the President?

LIPSEY: January? Wait, I'm trying to get my dates straight. Yeah. It must have been January, '74. Right.

Q: Did you in a similar capacity participate in the re-interment of the president's body when they moved it?

LIPSEY: Yeah. I helped them pick up the President's body and laid it in the casket.

Q: No, I'm talking about the subsequent to the funeral in 1963. I'm talking about years later.

LIPSEY: Oh. This is the first time I've discussed this – what I've discussed with you.

Q: No, you misunderstand the question. As you may recall, they hadn't finished the final resting place at Arlington National Cemetery.

LIPSEY: Oh, I'm sorry. At Arlington. When I left Washington he was still buried where the little gas light was on the side of the hill.

Q: So you do not recall him being moved into the permanent site which was very close to the original site? Did you participate in that?

LIPSEY: No, I do not.

Q: Do you know if Gen Wehle did?

LIPSEY: Obviously, he must have. Yes, because Gen Wehle was, if it was within the length – span when he was still in the service and he was still there well over a year about there after I left.

Q: Was here there after…

LIPSEY: Gen Wehle was there whenever anything was done as a formal nature and I'm sure that was a very formal thing. Gen Wehle was always there.

Q: But you don't specifically recall when it occurred?

LIPSEY: No, I really don't.

Q: Is there anything else about the autopsy or the evidence which came from the autopsy or about the people who were present?

LIPSEY: The only thing .and there once again, I'm sorry, this is the best I can tell you.

SECTION 2

LIPSEY: And once again, and I'm sorry, the best I can tell you is my recollection after all these years and obviously some speculation on my part.

The only thing, and it's certainly not going to hold up under any court of law-type thing. But, I can remember when the Warren Commission was formed. Everybody's writing books about it. All the comments on how many times he was shot and the angles. I remember Walter Cronkite doing this big CBS thing on who shot him – how many directions it came from. I can remember vividly in my mind on literally hundreds of occasions, saying these people are crazy. I watched the autopsy and I know for a fact he was shot three times. And the doctors were firmly convinced they all came out of the same gun because of the type of wounds or the entrances, whatever. I wish I could be more specific. I remember going back to the autopsy. I can remember specifically the next week, the next month. Over the period of the next year or so. Which was when I really remember what went on in the room. These people were crazy.

I can remember in my own mind, they're trying to read something into it that didn't happen. One book came out that he was shot from three different angles, another report came out he was only shot once, another that he was shot seven times. All kinds of… Everybody had their own versions of what happened, how many sounds they heard, and the angles of the fire they came from. I definitely remember the doctors commenting they were convinced that the shots came from the same direction and from the same type of weapon – and it was three shots.

Q: Did they also feel – did the doctors state that three separate bullets had struck?

LIPSEY: This is one other thing, that to the best of my memory, today, and remembering what I thought about when all these reports came out absolutely, unequivocally yes, they were convinced that he had been shot three times.

Q: It's unclear to me from the sketch that you did where there are three bullets.

LIPSEY: One on the right side of his head, one on the upper point of his neck and one on the lower part of his neck.

Q: Well, on your sketch, you labeled two points as points of entrance.

LIPSEY: One point was just blown away. This point was just blown away. I just can't remember whether there was a point of entrance and then the blown away part or whether it – he must have been sitting like this and it hit like this and went in just blew that away or if it ripped the whole section away.

Q: Either of those two possibilities means one bullet to the head, I think.

LIPSEY: Right. One bullet to the head.

Q: Right.

LIPSEY: Then one bullet to the lower head.

Q: Oh. Then where did that bullet exit?

LIPSEY: That's the bullet that exited right here.

Q: The throat.

LIPSEY: Throat. Then the lower entrance that did not exit. If that's confusing, ask me again and we'll go over it. Do you understand it? What I'm talking about so far? One bullet, right on his head. The bullet was coming out like this –

Q: The question is, the bullet wound that you're referring to right hand side of his head,

LIPSEY: Right.

Q: Did that, did this wound, which you describe as a large blasting out, did that have a separate corresponding entry wound or did the doctors believe that was all of one wound?

LIPSEY: That was all part of one wound.

Q: Could it have been part of that lower wound on the head that you labeled?

LIPSEY: Oh no. Absolutely not.

Q: Because, earlier when I asked you about the blown away portion, I go the impression that when you were saying you weren't sure whether it entered and then blew away a portion or whether the entrance and exit were part of the same hole.

LIPSEY: You're right. I wasn't. This was distinctly a separate wound beside, in relation to these two.

Q: Did the doctors conclude [laughing] that was there a two separate wounds was there a track between the two of them?

LIPSEY: The doctors concluded, the conclusion of the doctors was there were three separate wounds.

Q: And three separate bullets.

LIPSEY: And three separate bullets. No question in my mind about that. Can I ask you a question at this point?

Q: You can ask us but we may not be able to answer it for you.

LIPSEY: I think it will be a very simple question that I think you could answer. There's gotta be something to do with it. Why don't they exhume the body and study the body?

Q: We'll that's a question we can't answer.

LIPSEY: You can't answer that? [Incredulous]

Q: That's a policy judgement.

LIPSEY: Okay, that 's a policy judgement. It's gotta clear up a lot of things. I just can't imagine why they just don't go shriiiittt [whistling sound] I remember the discussion when, Lyndon Johnson said, "This body," you know, "none of the details of the Warren Report and this body will not be touched for..." what was it? 15, 20 years? Whatever? I remember he came out in public and made that statement, but I don't remember. I'm just curious why they don't dig him up if it's so vitally concerned about it instead of wasting you guy's time?

Q: On this sketch could you add a further identification where you say "part blown away." That's my confusion.

LIPSEY: Okay. [writing and speaking out loud] Entrance of bullet #2 and entrance of bullet #3.

Q: When you say "wound #1, why don't you say…

Q: [All speaking at once] That, to you, represents entrance of bullet #1.

LIPSEY: That would represent… No. Not in sequence. The bullet #1 may have been this bullet and that may have been #2. I don't remember the sequence.

Q: Of course. But for the purpose of this paper, that could be the sequence.

LIPSEY: [writing and speaking out loud] Entrance and exit –

Q: Entrance and exit.

LIPSEY: Exit of bullet #1. This would be entrance of bullet #2. Entrance of bullet #3. Not in order.

Q: Just write "For identification."

LIPSEY: [writing and speaking out loud] For identification. This same area blown away as…

Q: Wound #1.

LIPSEY: [writing and speaking out loud] Wound #1. [then different notation] Exit point of wound #2.

Q: Now, let me ask you this to clear up, I think we stated this explicitly, but, the point on the sketch labeled as point on entrance wound #2, did you in fact see that hole?

LIPSEY: All I saw was when they turned him over on his side, we took him out of the boxed coffin that they brought him from the hospital, he was laying on his back, they laid him on the table. When I saw him is when they turned him on his side and I saw it from a distance of 20ft, 15ft I saw the big blood area. I did not get any closer look at the hole than that.

Q: But [tape missing a few words] of the doctor.

LIPSEY: [writing and speaking out loud] [writing and speaking out loud] And what I could see relatively from where I was sitting that's about the position of it. Yes.

Q: So essentially, the doctors said there were two bullet wounds to the head. Is that correct?

LIPSEY: Not really, not considering if you want to consider this a head or a neck wound. I consider it more of a neck wound and I believe in their discussions they discussed it more of a neck wound. I consider my wound #1 is the head wound. I consider this wound #2 on a Upper neck/lower part of your head

Q: Was it in the hair, hairline?

LIPSEY: Yes. It was in the hair, but the lower hairline.

Q: It was in the hair?

LIPSEY: Just a minute. Wait. I'm considering where my hairline is today. Like I say, it was just a blood smash area back there. It could have been in the part that you sort of shave right up there. But lower head still, but upper neck. But the third one definitely was the lower neck, upper vertebrae.

At this time we'll have to stop.
The time is 1:00 and I'll insert another tape.
The time is 1:03 – we're starting this tape.

LIPSEY: Are ya'll drawing conclusions after you've done your thing for a couple of years? Or are you going to bound it up and keep it for future reference.

Q: ...the committee will make it public.

LIPSEY: Are you, so...if, I can ask you this, you're concerned more, obviously, with just talking with me and other people about the autopsy and whatever, your investigation I presume, covers the whole realm of the assassination...

Q: We're investigating the assassination generally.

LIPSEY: Generally, conspiracy, whatever, you're investigating the whole thing. Obviously, I know nothing about that. I was just curious. I guess everybody in the whole world is curious since Oswald was killed, and then Ruby was killed. There's something rotten in Denmark, obviously, somewhere. I don't know that we will ever find out.

Q to Q: If you are preceding away from the issue – away from the wounds... do you have any questions?

Q: Do you remember whether or not during the autopsy any skull fragments were brought into the room?

LIPSEY: No. I don't think there were. I think I might have remembered if they brought any other parts of the body in there. I don't, uh, not at all.

118

Q: Pertaining to a pre-autopsy, how did you determine where the autopsy would be, at Bethesda?

LIPSEY: We were told where to take the body to. We immediately got back to our offices about 1:00 that afternoon. General Wehle called the White House and spoke to our liaison officer or whoever it happened to be at that time. Gen Wehle. spoke to them at length. Then we would have little plan of a funeral, when you start planning funerals what needs to be in Washington. And then it was communicated to us it would be an autopsy performed. First they indicated to us the autopsy they would perform it in Dallas. And then somebody up the chain of command, like the White House, or at some higher level than us, said no, not in Dallas. Would do it in Washington and then, where. And then it was decided it was to be done at Bethesda Naval Station.

[Talks about helicopter ride] to make a side comment, I remember never being so frightened in my life. We took off from Andrews Airforce base in one of those – oh, I forget the number of it. You may or may not remember those banana-shaped helicopters, those long – they were shaped like a banana with a rotor on both ends, huge things, held about 30-40 people. They had the reputation of being not very safe. And can I remember they loaded that thing up and it was pitch black dark outside I just happen to remember because I flew in and out of Washington a lot and all those planes that used to land at National. Every 30 seconds there's a plane landing. I remember taking off in that damn thing and flying across Washington. Everything entered my mind imaginable. It was loaded. We had the honor guard in that thing with us. All the seats were taken up. We had two Lt.'s flying the thing who were younger than I was and I was young. I was scared to death.

[Interrupted by intercom.]

I can remember being frightened flying across there. Just in that damn thing, it's pitch black outside and wondering whose telling other planes there are helicopters flying over Washington. Then we went to land at the hospital. They had the helipad where helicopters land. In numbers, I don't know there looked to over several thousand people on the ground – there was no place to land. I remember looking out the window and the police forcing the people back. There were lights on the ground. They got the crowd back far enough so we could set that helicopter down. If the wind had been blowing strongly one way or another or he had slipped one quarter of an inch, or that plane had tilted one eighth of an inch, exaggerating, of course, we'd cut off four thousand people's heads. That kid landed that helicopter right in the middle of this humongus crowd. I know he had been scared to death too. There was no room or margin for error when he set that helicopter down. Three feet one way or the other and he'd set that helicopter down in the crowd...I've flown all my life, storms, I've flown in tornadoes, in an airplane.

Q: Delta airlines. [evidently referring to a plaque or award from Delta Airlines in Lipsey's office.]

LIPSEY: Yeah, I fly in airplanes so doggoned much. They gave it to me for flying their airlines so darn much. I've been scared in airplanes. I guess everybody does. I just had visions landing that helicopter in all those people.

Q: I've got one last question. After the autopsy, you mentions materials were retained from the body physically. Evidence, photographs and x-rays

LIPSEY: Wehle never saw them, to my knowledge and I never saw them.

Q: So, you had no further – never had custody.

LIPSEY: Never saw them. None whatsoever. Our obligation as far as the autopsy ended right there. I'm not sure we had any obligation for the autopsy except Gen Wehle was responsible for the funeral. Gen. Wehle, he wanted somebody there to make sure nobody carted that body off until he could get back there and till everything was taken to the White House. He said, "You stay here and watch it."

I'm sorry I couldn't be more help to you. It's been a long time. Like I said, the three entrance wounds and the only thing I remember vividly because of my listening to comments immediately after all these reports began coming out. Obviously, I really wasn't interested in the autopsy, quite frankly, I was more interested in looking at pictures of the man and at the time – really planning the funeral. At the time I wanted to study. I wanted to be up there with Gen Wehle wondering what the plans were [rather] than sitting in that room. That's the best I can tell you.

Obviously, everything I've told you here. First of all, I've never discussed any part of the autopsy with anybody. You are the first I have discussed it with – not even with my wife. And the thing, relating back to the thing, it had to do with National Security, more as I had a Top Secret rating – because I was exposed to every Top Secret document in Washington. I briefed the President with Gen. Wehle and things. And, of course, that had more to do with, we signed those, we would not discuss... I feel like it was, it had more to do with relating to the president and his dealings, or at the time what his plans were, or any of the people he had talked to or confidentiality, or anything read that came from our office to his office. Still, I felt that if it should be told to anyone, it should be told to authorized persons such as yourself. For that reason, and Gen Wehle and I kind of agreed we would never discuss it among ourselves. It's never been discussed with anybody. And I certainly would not want my comments made public. I don't think they should be.

Q: Okay, you have the card that Andy gave you with the Committee address and telephone number and if you need to contact us you can call collect.

LIPSEY: I appreciate it. If I think of anything else, I'd certainly be glad to tell you. That's why I never got real excited and never called anybody to come see me because really, my part was dealing with ,it was meeting Kings and Queens and presidents that came, getting to meet them all. I've got them all written down – 62 Kings and Queens, or pres. of foreign countries. And it was a heck of an exciting experience while we were there. We were in charge of, if you remember, the March on Washington in August of that year. That was an exciting time. We got to do so many exciting things. But more ours were functional exciting things. Of course, being the funeral, we started this thing on Friday at noon and didn't go to bed till Monday night. We went back to our rooms just to change clothes.

Q: I'll terminate the tape at this time. It's now 1:13.

end

Index

Acknowledgments

It's been almost 53 years since the assassination of John F Kennedy. For 47 of those years, my wife Beryl,has been by my side. Life would be meaningless without her. As well, our daughter, Kelli, has been a source of great love and joy to me. You were, and are, the apple of my eye, sweetheart.

My mother and father, James and Rachel Clark, have been gone many years. But I know they would be proud of my accomplishments in life, and it's all due to the way they showed me and my brothers and sisters kindness, love, and discipline.

My brothers, sisters, and I, have always been close, and my life would not have been the same without them, aka: the 12th Avenue Gang: James jr., Samuel, Alberta, Ben, Evangeline, Joe, Mary, Henrietta, Louis,and Francis . My thanks to Phil Singer, and William Law for bringing me and my honor guard Brothers together again after 51 years at the conference in Westmont Illinois They are: Tim Cheek, and James Felder. Those who could not be with us at the conference but were there in spirit, Bud Barnum, Richard Gaudreau, Doug Mayfield, the late Larry Smith, Jerry Diamond, and the late Samuel Bird. I would also like to acknowledge Richard lipsey, who flew with us aboard the helicopter to Bethesda Naval Hospital on the night of November 22nd 1963, and my new friends Dennis David, James Jenkins, and James Metzler. Their knowledge of events that night at Bethesda Naval Hospital has changed my life.

I would also like to acknowledge Lori Michelle Law. Lori typed the manuscript, and made many helpful suggestions along the way. My thanks as well to Patsy Huey, who read a late draft of the manuscript and also made corrections.

My publisher at TrineDay publishing, Kris Millegan, deserves special thanks, for asking me to take on this project. Kris specialises in publishing subjects that no other publisher will touch.

It is with much gratitude that I thank St John Hunt, son of the late E.Howard Hunt, for his gracious and thoughtful foreword to this book. It is through his efforts, and many more like him, that the JFK mystery may one day be solved.

I would also like to acknowledge my closest friend for the last 60 years, Ronnie La Land.

I would also like to acknowledge the Atlanta VA Medical Center and they're fine nursing staff.

– Hugh Clark, September 2016

Dr. Mary's Monkey

How the Unsolved Murder of a Doctor, a Secret Laboratory in New Orleans and Cancer-Causing Monkey Viruses are Linked to Lee Harvey Oswald, the JFK Assassination and Emerging Global Epidemics

BY EDWARD T. HASLAM, FOREWORD BY JIM MARRS

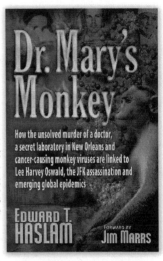

Evidence of top-secret medical experiments and cover-ups of clinical blunders
The 1964 murder of a nationally known cancer researcher sets the stage for this gripping exposé of medical professionals enmeshed in covert government operations over the course of three decades. Following a trail of police records, FBI files, cancer statistics, and medical journals, this revealing book presents evidence of a web of medical secret-keeping that began with the handling of evidence in the JFK assassination and continued apace, sweeping doctors into cover-ups of cancer outbreaks, contaminated polio vaccine, the genesis of the AIDS virus, and biological weapon research using infected monkeys.

Softcover: **$19.95** (ISBN: 9781634240307) • 432 pages • Size: 5 1/2 x 8 1/2
Hardcover: **$24.95** (ISBN: 9781937584597)

Me & Lee

How I Came to Know, Love and Lose Lee Harvey Oswald

BY JUDYTH VARY BAKER

FOREWORD BY EDWARD T. HASLAM

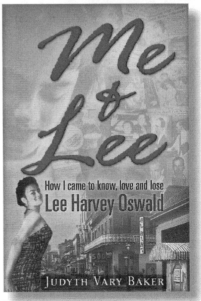

JUDYTH VARY WAS ONCE A PROMISING science student who dreamed of finding a cure for cancer; this exposé is her account of how she strayed from a path of mainstream scholarship at the University of Florida to a life of espionage in New Orleans with Lee Harvey Oswald. In her narrative she offers extensive documentation on how she came to be a cancer expert at such a young age, the personalities who urged her to relocate to New Orleans, and what lead to her involvement in the development of a biological weapon that Oswald was to smuggle into Cuba to eliminate Fidel Castro. Details on what she knew of Kennedy's impending assassination, her conversations with Oswald as late as two days before the killing, and her belief that Oswald was a deep-cover intelligence agent who was framed for an assassination he was actually trying to prevent, are also revealed.

JUDITH VARY BAKER is a teacher, and artist. Edward T. Haslam is the author of *Dr. Mary's Monkey*.

Hardcover • $24.95 • Softrcover • $21.95 ISBN 9780979988677 / 978-1936296378 • 608 Pages

A Secret Order
Investigating the High Strangeness and Synchronicity in the JFK Assassination
by H. P. Albarelli, Jr.

Provocative new theories that uncover coincidences, connections, and unexplained details of the JFK assassination

Reporting new and never-before-published information about the assassination of John F. Kennedy, this investigation dives straight into the deep end, and seeks to prove the CIA's involvement in one of the most controversial topics in American history. Featuring intelligence gathered from CIA agents who reported their involvement in the assassination, the case is broken wide open while covering unexplored ground. Gritty details about the assassination are interlaced throughout, while primary and secondary players to the murder are revealed in the in-depth analysis. Although a tremendous amount has been written in the nearly five decades since the assassination, there has never been, until now, a publication to explore the aspects of the case that seemed to defy explanation or logic.

H. P. ALBARELLI JR. is an author and reporter whose previous works can be found in the Huffington Post, Pravda, and Counterpunch. His 10-year investigation into the death of biochemist Dr. Frank Olson was featured on A&E's Investigative Reports, and is the subject of his book, A Terrible Mistake. He lives in Indian Beach, Florida.

Softcover • **$24.95** • ISBN 9781936296552 • 469 Pages

Survivor's Guilt
The Secret Service and the Failure to Protect President Kennedy
by Vincent Michael Palamara

The actions and inactions of the Secret Service before, during, and after the Kennedy assassination

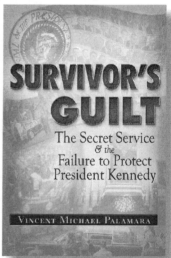

Painstakingly researched by an authority on the history of the Secret Service and based on primary, firsthand accounts from more than 80 former agents, White House aides, and family members, this is the definitive account of what went wrong with John F. Kennedy's security detail on the day he was assassinated.

The work provides a detailed look at how JFK could and should have been protected and debunks numerous fraudulent notions that persist about the day in question, including that JFK ordered agents off the rear of his limousine; demanded the removal of the bubble top that covered the vehicle; and was difficult to protect and somehow, directly or indirectly, made his own tragic death easier for an assassin or assassins. This book also thoroughly investigates the threats on the president's life before traveling to Texas; the presence of unauthorized Secret Service agents in Dealey Plaza, the site of the assassination; the failure of the Secret Service in monitoring and securing the surrounding buildings, overhangs, and rooftops; and the surprising conspiratorial beliefs of several former agents.

An important addition to the canon of works on JFK and his assassination, this study sheds light on the gross negligence and, in some cases, seeming culpability, of those sworn to protect the president.

Vincent Michael Palamara is an expert on the history of the Secret Service. He has appeared on the History Channel, C-SPAN, and numerous newspapers and journals, and his original research materials are stored in the National Archives. He lives in Pittsburgh, Pennsylvania.

Softcover • **$24.95** • ISBN 9781937584603 • 492 Pages

In the Eye of History
Disclosures in the JFK Assassination Medical Evidence
SECOND EDITION
BY WILLIAM MATSON LAW

An oral history of the JFK autopsy

Anyone interested in the greatest mystery of the 20th century will benefit from the historic perspective of the attendees of President Kennedy's autopsy. For the first time in their own words these witnesses to history give firsthand accounts of what took place in the autopsy morgue at Bethesda, Maryland, on the night on November 22, 1963. Author William Matson Law set out on a personal quest to reach an understanding of the circumstances underpinning the assassination of John F. Kennedy. His investigation led him to the autopsy on the president's body at the National Naval Medical Center. In the Eye of History comprises conversations with eight individuals who agreed to talk: Dennis David, Paul O'Connor, James Jenkins, Jerrol Custer, Harold Rydberg, Saundra Spencer, and ex-FBI Special Agents James Sibert and Frances O'Neill. These eyewitnesses relate their stories comprehensively, and Law allows them to tell it as they remember it without attempting to fit any pro- or anticonspiracy agenda. The book also features a DVD featuring these firsthand interviews. Comes with DVD.

Softcover: **$29.95** (ISBN: 9781634240468) • 514 pages • Size: 6 x 9

JFK from Parkland to Bethesda
The Ultimate Kennedy Assassination Compendium
BY VINCENT PALAMARA

An all-in-one resource containing more than 15 years of research on the JFK assassination

A map through the jungle of statements, testimony, allegations, and theories relating to the assassination of John F. Kennedy, this compendium gives readers an all-in-one resource for facts from this intriguing slice of history. The book, which took more than 15 years to research and write, includes details on all of the most important aspects of the case, including old and new medical evidence from primary and secondary sources. JFK: From Parkland to Bethesda tackles the hard evidence of conspiracy and cover-up and presents a mass of sources and materials, making it an invaluable reference for anyone with interest in the President Kennedy and his assassination in 1963.

Softcover: **$19.95** (ISBN: 9781634240277) • 242 pages • Size: 6 x 9

The Polka Dot File on the Robert F. Kennedy Killing
Paris Peace Talks connection
BY FERNANDO FAURA

"THE POLKA DOT FILE IS A GEM IN THE FIELD OF RFK ASSASSINATION RESEARCH. READ IT AND LEARN."
—JIM DOUGLASS, AUTHOR, *JFK AND THE UNSPEAKABLE*

The Polka Dot File on the Robert F. Kennedy Killing describes the day-to-day chase for the mystery woman in the polka-dot dress. The book comments on but does not dwell on the police investigation, and reads like a detective thriller instead of an academic analysis of the investigation. It incorporates actual tapes made by an important witness, and introduces the testimony of witnesses not covered in other books and it is a new take on the assassination and the motives for it introduces a new theory for the reasons behind the assassination. Original and highly personal, it reaches a startling and different conclusion not exposed by other books.

FERNANDO FAURA graduated cum laude with a degree in journalism from the California State University. In 1967 he joined *The Hollywood Citizens News.* Fernando has won awards from the Press Club, the National Newspaper Publishers Association, and was nominated for a Pulitzer Prize.

Softcover: **$24.95** (ISBN: 9781634240598) • 248 pages • Size: 6 x 9

From an Office Building with a High-Powered Rifle

A report to the public from an FBI agent involved in the official JFK assassination investigation

by Don Adams

An insider's look at the mysteries behind the death of President Kennedy

The personal and professional story of a former FBI agent, this is the journey Don Adams has taken over the past 50 years that has connected him to the assassination of the 35th president of the United States. On November 13, 1963, Adams was given a priority assignment to investigate Joseph Milteer, a man who had made threats to assassinate the president. Two weeks later John F. Kennedy was dead, and Agent Adams was instructed to locate and question Milteer. Adams, however, was only allowed to ask the suspect five specific questions before being told to release him. He was puzzled by the bizarre orders but thought nothing more of it until years later when he read a report that stated that not only had Joseph Milteer made threats against the president, but also that he claimed Kennedy would be killed from an office building with a high-powered rifle. Since that time, Adams has compiled evidence and research from every avenue available to him, including his experiences in Georgia and Dallas FBI offices, to produce this compelling investigation that may just raise more questions than answers.

DON ADAMS is a former FBI agent who participated in the investigation of the assassination of John F. Kennedy. He is the author of numerous articles on the subject and is considered a respected authority on the topic. He lives in Akron, Ohio.

Softcover • $24.95 • ISBN 9781936296866 • 236 Pages

Self-Portrait of a Scoundrel

by Chauncey Holt

A Kennedy insider steps out of the shadows with a riveting account of his life and escapades

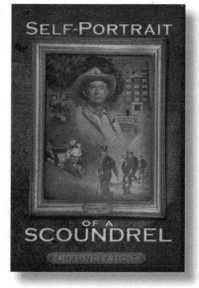

Released for the first time 16 years after his death, this startling autobiography by one of the so-called "three tramps" from the John F. Kennedy assassination reveals the details of Chauncey Marvin Holt's many claims. Much mystery and suspicion still swirls around that fateful day in November 1963, and theories abound in nearly every form of media. But one of the major mysteries revolves around the three men spotted and later arrested in Dealey Plaza. Holt's controversial confession to being one of the three tramps has a history of its own, and in his own words he delves into his unique and wild background and life. From his United States Air Force service during Pearl Harbor to his associations with the mob and the CIA, Holt discusses his experiences and encounters in great detail. From a man who truly lived a rare and unique life, the book explains the ins and outs of his associations with Lee Harvey Oswald and the assassination in this unique retrospective of a complex and occasionally dubious life.

CHAUNCEY HOLT came forward claiming to be one of the "three tramps" photographed in Dealey Plaza shortly after the assassination of President John F. Kennedy. At various times in his life, he claimed to be a CIA operative, an accountant for Meyer Lansky, and ostensibly provided false ID documents to Lee Harvey Oswald.

Softcover • $24.95 • ISBN 9781937584375 • 622 Pages

A Rose by Many Other Names
Rose Cherami & the JFK Assassination

by Todd C. Elliott

A look into the "birthplace" of the JFK conspiracy

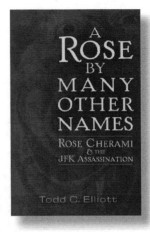

Shifting the focus away from the assassination of John F. Kennedy in Dealey Plaza in Dallas, Texas, to 48 hours prior in Eunice, Louisiana, this book explores the prediction made by Melba Marcades, aka Rose Cherami, that the president would be assassinated on Friday, November 22, 1963 in Dallas. Discounting clairvoyance, the book investigates the possibility that Rose had inside information about the assassination. However, Rose Cherami was not a credible witness: she was a prostitute, a one-time performer in Jack Ruby's Carousel Club, an admitted drug trafficker, a drug addict, and a car thief. But the author's research reveals glaring omissions in her FBI files, questionable admissions regarding her criminal history, and the dubious details of her untimely demise. This book sheds new light on a relatively unknown footnote of the JFK conspiracy theory.

TODD C. ELLIOTT is a former AM talk radio host and a freelance writer and journalist whose work has been featured in the Abbeville Meridian, American Press, the Crowley Post-Signal, the Daily Advertiser, the Eunice News, the Jambalaya News, Lagniappe Magazine, and the Public News. He lives in Lake Charles, Louisiana.

Softcover • **$12.95** • ISBN 9781937584634 • 98 Pages

Bond of Secrecy
My Life With CIA Spy and Watergate Conspirator E. Howard Hunt

by Saint John Hunt

Foreword by Jesse Ventura

Afterword by Eric Hamburg

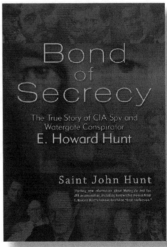

Sometime after midnight June 17, 1972, I was catapulted out of a deep sleep when the stygian darkness of my basement room was shattered by a shaft of light. My father, silhouetted in the doorway, was calling to me. "Saint, Saint John! Wake up!" He flicked on my light and stepped quickly to the center of the room. I sat upright and looked questioningly at my father, slowly focusing on his face. He was perspiring heavily and seemed extremely agitated. His breathing was quick and shallow as he talked in short bursts, pausing to search for the right words. At that early morning hour in the darkness of my bedroom, I had no way of knowing that this moment would forever change my life. For our family and so many others the world was about to turn upside down, and there would begin a bond of secrecy between my father and me that would last 35 years.

A father's last confession to his son about the CIA, Watergate, and the plot to assassinate President John F. Kennedy, this is the remarkable true story of St. John Hunt and his father E. Howard Hunt, the infamous Watergate burglar and CIA spymaster. In Howard Hunt's near-death confession to his son St. John, he revealed that key figures in the CIA were involved in the plot to assassinate JFK in Dallas, and that Hunt himself was approached by the plotters, who included the CIA's David Atlee Phillips, Cord Meyer, Jr., and William Harvey, as well as future Watergate burglar Frank Sturgis. An incredible true story told from an inside, authoritative source, this is also a personal account of a uniquely dysfunctional American family caught up in two of the biggest political scandals of the 20th century.

SAINT JOHN HUNT was born in 1954 in Washington, DC, lived with his family in Tokyo 1955-58, in Montevideo, Uruguay 1958-62 and from 1962-66 in Spain, Mexico City and the U.S.

In 1970 his father told him that he had worked for the CIA and OSS since WWII. In 1972 his father was arrested for Watergate and his mother Dorothy was killed in a plane crash.

A musician, Saint John spent the next 35 years working in various rock bands and raising two children. Currently he is working as a musician.

Softcover • **$24.95** • ISBN 9781936296835 • 192 Pages

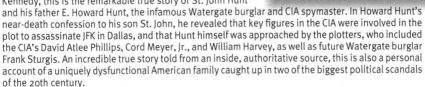

David Ferrie
Mafia Pilot, Participant in Anti-Castro Bioweapon Plot, Friend of Lee Harvey Oswald and Key to the JFK Assassination
by Judyth Vary Baker

One of the more eccentric characters linked to the JFK assassination

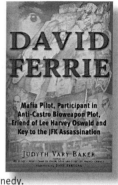

Of the all the people surrounding the assassination of President Kennedy, few are more mysterious and enigmatic than David William Ferrie of New Orleans. Author Judyth Vary Baker knew David Ferrie personally and worked with him in a covert project in New Orleans during the summer of 1963, and this book examines his strange and puzzling behavior both before and after the assassination. At the time of the assassination, Ferrie was a 45-year-old New Orleans resident who was acquainted with some of the most notorious names linked to the assassination: Lee Oswald, Clay Shaw, Guy Banister, Jack Ruby, and Carlos Marcello. He possessed assorted talents and eccentricities: he was at one time a senior pilot with Eastern Airlines until he was fired for homosexual activity on the job; he was also a hypnotist; a serious researcher of the origins of cancer; an amateur psychologist; and a victim of a strange disease, alopecia, which made all of his body void of hair. His odd lifestyle was embellished with an equally bizarre appearance featuring a red toupee and false eyebrows. This is the first book focused solely on David Ferrie and his alleged involvement in the conspiracy to assassinate President John F. Kennedy.

JUDYTH VARY BAKER is an artist, writer, and poet who first became known as a young prodigy in cancer research, then, later, for her assertion that while conducting cancer research in New Orleans in the summer of 1963, she had a love affair with Lee Harvey Oswald. She is the author of *Me & Lee: How I Came to Know, Love and Lose Lee Harvey Oswald*. She lives in Europe.

Softcover • **$24.95** • ISBN 9781937584542 • 528 Pages

LBJ and the Kennedy Killing
By Eyewitness
James T. Tague

This is unlike any other book about the assassination of President John F. Kennedy. The author, James Tague, was there and he was wounded by the debris from a missed shot on that fateful day. He stood up to our Government when the Warren Commission was about to ignore what really happened and spoke to the true facts. James Tague's testimony changed history and the "magic bullet" was born in an effort by the Warren Commission to wrongly explain all the wounds to President Kennedy and Governor Connally, and to try and convince the public that Lee Harvey Oswald was the "lone nut assassin." Tague, a long time Dallas area resident, initially believed the Warren Report, but time, diligent research and amazing revelations told to him by prominent Texans has given James Tague an inside look at what really happened. Be prepared to learn new facts, never before published, about one of our nation's darkest moments.

JAMES T. TAGUE spent 5 years in the Air Force, had a career in the automobile business rising to top management and is today recognized as a top researcher on the Kennedy assassination. It was an accident of timing that he was in Dealey Plaza that November day in 1963, receiving a minor injury.

Softcover • **$29.95** • ISBN 9781937584740 • 433 Pages

Kennedy & Oswald   *–The Big Picture–*
by Judyth Vary Baker and Edward Schwartz

Unraveling the many strands of hidden history behind the assassination of President Kennedy is not an easy task. Co-authors Baker and Schwartz guide us toward the conclusion that ultimately, the motivation was total governmental control, a coup d'état, changing us from a democratic republic to a oligopoly – a corporatocracy. With help from new witnesses regarding the "Crime of the Century," we are led to the realization that the "War of Terror" and the Patriot Act were predesigned to undermine our US Constitution and our Bill of Rights. The very moment Kennedy died our own government turned against "We the People." Baker and Schwartz provide a compelling narrative showing Oswald's innocence and a condemnation of the conspirators who planned and carried out the assassination of our 35th president and our Republic.

Softcover • **$24.95** • ISBN 9781634240963 • 408 Pages

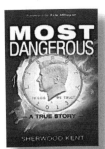

Most Dangerous   *–A True Story–*
by Sherwood Kent

OUT OF THE BOWELS of the sleepy southern town of Tupelo, Mississippi, the birthplace of Elvis Presley, emerges a darkly-humorous true story of staged terror, occult ritual and mind control. The book reads like a Faulkneresque tall tale but is, unfortunately for the main character and those around him, all-too-true.

Author S.K. Bain finds himself caught up in the middle of something bigger and uglier than he can at first fathom. Yet, much to his dismay, he catches on rather quickly to what's taking place around him—and near-simultaneously elsewhere across the county in places such as Boston, MA and West, TX—because he's seen this sort of thing before. He wrote the book on it, literally, and he soon realizes just how much danger he and his family are in.

The year is 2013, the 50th anniversary of the JFK assassination, and Bain discovers that he is enmeshed in a year-long series of scripted events meticulously planned and brilliantly executed by some of the most ruthless, diabolically-creative, powerful psychopaths on the planet. As the story unfolds, it turns out that Bain has an idea who, specifically, might be behind his woes, and if he's correct, it's even less likely that he's going to get out alive.

Softcover • **$24.95** • ISBN 9781634240406 • 408 Pages

Sinister Forces
A Grimoire of American Political Witchcraft
Book One: The Nine
BY PETER LEVENDA, FOREWORD BY JIM HOUGAN

A shocking alternative to the conventional views of American history.

The roots of coincidence and conspiracy in American politics, crime, and culture are examined in this book, exposing new connections between religion, political conspiracy, and occultism. From ancient American civilization and the mysterious mound builder culture to the Salem witch trials, the birth of Mormonism during a ritual of ceremonial magic by Joseph Smith, Jr., and Operations Paperclip and Bluebird. Fascinating details are revealed, including the bizarre world of "wandering bishops" who appear throughout the Kennedy assassinations; a CIA mind control program run amok in the United States and Canada; a famous American spiritual leader who had ties to Lee Harvey Oswald in the weeks and months leading up to the assassination of President Kennedy; and the "Manson secret.

Softcover: **$24.95** (ISBN 9780984185818) • 432 pages • Size: 6 x 9

Book Two: A Warm Gun
Readers are provided with strange parallels between supernatural forces such as shaminism, ritual magic, and cult practices, and contemporary interrogation techniques such as those used by the CIA under the general rubric of MK-ULTRA. Not a work of speculative history, this exposé is founded on primary source material and historical documents. Fascinating details on Nixon and the "Dark Tower," the Assassin cult and more recent Islamic terrorism, and the bizarre themes that run through American history from its discovery by Columbus to the political assassinations of the 1960s are revealed.

Softcover: **$24.95** (ISBN 9780984185825) • 392 pages • Size: 6 x 9

Book Three: The Manson Secret
The Stanislavski Method as mind control and initiation. Filmmaker Kenneth Anger and Aleister Crowley, Marianne Faithfull, Anita Pallenberg, and the Rolling Stones. Filmmaker Donald Cammell (Performance) and his father, CJ Cammell (the first biographer of Aleister Crowley), and his suicide. Jane Fonda and Bluebird. The assassination of Marilyn Monroe. Fidel Castro's Hollywood career. Jim Morrison and witchcraft. David Lynch and spiritual transformation. The technology of sociopaths. How to create an assassin. The CIA, MK-ULTRA and programmed killers.

Softcover: **$24.95** (ISBN 9780984185832) • 508 pages • Size: 6 x 9